Egypt and the Origin of Civilization

VindicationPress

Series:
Diffusionism and the Origins of Civilizations

Coming soon by the same author:
Anthology: Controversial Pasts and the Philosophy of History, Volume I
Anthology: Controversial Pasts and the Philosophy of History, Volume II

Egypt and the Origin of Civilization
The British School of Culture Diffusion, 1890s–1940s
Volume I

Joshua Smith

Published by VindicationPress, 2011.
© Joshua Smith 2011
All rights reserved, including the right to reproduce this book or portions thereof in any form whatsoever.

Manufactured and printed in the United States of America

Smith, Joshua D.
　Egypt and the origin of civilization: the british school of culture diffusion, 1890s-1940s / by Joshua D. Smith
Originally published: VindicationPress, 2011.
Includes bibliographical references and index.
1. Egypt-Civilization. 2. Anthropology-Transoceanic contacts. 3. Cultural Diffusion. I. Title. II. Title: The British school of culture diffusionism. III. Series: Diffusionism and the origins of civilizations

ISBN-13: 978-0615451787
ISBN-10: 0615451780

CONTENTS

PREFACE 7

Chapter

1. INTRODUCTION: ENTERING ANTHROPOLOGY. 11

2. THEORETICAL CONTEXT 26

3. ADOLPH BASTIAN: PSYCHIC UNITY 46

4. RIVERS' SOURCES 54

5. CULTURE MOVEMENT AND ADAPTATION . . 66

6. FROM EVOLUTIONISM TO STRUCTURAL-FUNCTIONALISM. 81

7. SYNTHESIS 93

8. FUNDING AND CONCLUSION 107

BIBLIOGRAPHY 121

INDEX. 139

Audentes fortuna iuvat.
Virgil
Aeneid, book X, line 284

PREFACE

THE BRITISH SCHOOL OF CULTURE DIFFUSION: 1890s-1940s

This book intends to analyze the early developments and ultimate demise of a British school of anthropological thought and the grand theories of three anthropologists regarding culture diffusion. The proponents of the Heliolithic (literally meaning the words "sun" and "stones" denoting the solar or Heliocentric focus of the megalithic monument builders) school of diffusion, Grafton Elliot Smith, W. H. R. Rivers, and W. J. Perry, were each considered experts in their respective fields of science and research studies. Their wide-ranging claims were to play an important part in the emergence of a variety of interpretations for culture change in the newly forming discipline of anthropology in the movement towards professionalization of the field.

Relevant questions are addressed by an investigation into the primary source materials of the publications of Smith, Rivers, and Perry. The thesis of this volume contends that the British form of diffusionism did not develop to fruition due to truncated funding as the structural-functionalist theories in anthropology garnered greater financial support. This led to the provisional and temporary demise of both social evolutionism and diffusionism as totalizing explanatory schemes for the emergence and spread of civilization as they were subsumed within other schools of thought.

The early developments in the history of anthropology are significant to investigate because, at the turn of the 20th century, the field was still one of contested theoretical boundaries which, to a limited extent, remains to be the case today. The British school of diffusionism can be seen to have played a significant role in the emergence of the professional fields of ethnology and anthropology. Moreover, by analyzing the contributions of Smith, Rivers, and Perry, one may also note the academic overlap that occurred before anthropology was set upon the path of increasing specialization in terms of research and theory. For example, they performed research that gathered information from the fields of archeology, linguistics, physical anthropology, comparative mythology and comparative religion, Egyptology, ethnography, ethnology, and prehistory.

These events in British social anthropology are relevant to anyone researching the establishment of academic fields as specialized, professionalized disciplines. This work will also attempt to answer the following questions: Why did the search for the origins of civilization lead to what is today judged to have been such a misguided theory of cultural change?, Why was the Heliolithic school not immediately removed from the arena of legitimate debate within anthropology?, What was the role of the academic community?, finally, What led to the demise of this theory of wide-ranging cultural diffusion? Additionally, these questions are relevant in a more general sense to historical inquiry because they seek to determine how a few aspects regarding academic fields over time establish what is and is not acceptable for legitimate scholarly debate.

Furthermore, the primary source materials offer critical observations which were noted by the advocates themselves. For example, Rivers seemed most prescient when he addressed potential problems with then current dating methods that he believed could overturn their theory of trait diffusion from Egypt, which radiocarbon dating later did in some ways. There were also links between their theories of culture and their political ideas that are relevant to this study. In addition, the work of contemporary commentators, ethnologists, anthropologists (including archeologists), Egyptologists, and prehistorians will provide material for the depth of the numerous debates of the time. These sources should provide a bit of information on the socio-political and economic context of the age and the implications of the competing theories of the time. Furthermore, a number of secondary sources of importance have commented upon the early debates about the British school of diffusion. These almost invariably do not treat the subject in a respectful manner and are often off-handedly dismissive and derisive in tone. This is not a very productive approach to take when aiming for a measure of objectivity in analysis.

Regarding the interpretation of the events, this author shall withhold from the openly condemnatory approach to the British school of diffusionists that has become common since the late 1940s in order to provide balance to the debate. Such blatant hostility is not beneficial to historical inquiry. Instead, the focus will be upon demonstrating key connections between ideas of the day and the advocates of various ethnological and anthropological theories, which emerged throughout the process of debating the role of culture diffusion in culture change. Moreover, though objectivity is of importance in framing the theoretical context, it is not intended to impose a totalizing neutrality on every issue related to Heliolithic diffusionism.

Prior to the time of Smith, Rivers, and Perry, there had been a number of advocates of the notion that the Middle East was at the heart of the origin of civilization. Christianity inspired many such speculations and investigations and therefore, deserves some consideration for the possible role that these earlier conjectures may have influenced the advocates of a theory of diffusion centered in ancient Egypt. Many of these theories, however, were stridently non-academic and therefore will not carry the weight of the primary source commentaries, writings, and research of Smith, Rivers, and Perry but may be noted as prospective influences.

This text will also contend that the structural-functionalist theories in anthropology garnered greater financial support as they were deemed to be more useful in a utilitarian sense from the colonialist and post-colonialist interests. This, in turn, led to the demise of both social evolutionism and diffusionism as totalizing explanatory schemes for the emergence, development, and spread of civilization in the field of anthropology. Finally, this work is the initial entry in a projected multi-volume series of investigations into theories of diffusion, Pre-Columbian transoceanic contacts, the sociology of scientific knowledge, and the origins of civilizations.

Joshua Smith
March 2011

CHAPTER ONE

INTRODUCTION

ENTERING ANTHROPOLOGY

The British anthropological school of diffusionism, which proposed a special role in cultural development for ancient Egypt, emerged in the late 19th and early 20th centuries in the works of W.H.R. Rivers, W.J. Perry, and Grafton Elliot Smith. This school of thought witnessed its greatest period of prominence during the 1910s to early 1920s. It developed during a period of emergent conflict and transition between three main approaches to anthropological and ethnological theory: social evolutionism, diffusionism, and structural-functionalism.[1] Diffusion was also challenged by nativist isolationism (theories of exclusive indigenous development) that admitted of no transoceanic cultural contacts excepting those of European priority (Columbus, Vikings, and the like).[2] Recent literature treats the emergence of this school with dismay and lauds the demise of British diffusionist theory. This is particularly the case in works by authors who refer almost exclusively to secondary source material for their criticisms. Ultimately, the vast majority of critiques of diffusionism garner their information from histories of the discipline written by anthropologists (rather than historians) who are or were advocates of

---

[1] British diffusionism may be seen as a subcategory of the more generalized form of theoretical diffusionism. Another subcategory that existed around the same time was German diffusionism, which took a different form to be explained later.

[2] Martin Bernal, Black Athena: The Afroasiatic Roots of Classical Civilization, (New Brunswick, New Jersey: Rutgers University Press, 1991), v. II, 31, 225-226, 270-272.

either social evolutionism, structural-functionalism, processualism, cultural materialism, or post-processualism among others.

These attacks have obscured the fact that diffusionist versions of social anthropology were not without scholarly precursors in Britain and continental Europe. The Egyptocentric diffusion scheme proposed by these British scholars, however, did go further than most and suggested that the emergence of civilization was so unique and fortuitous an event that it could have emerged only once and in a single place. Subsequently, the diffusionists contended, Egypt passed on key innovations over time to peoples all over the world—but not through direct or intentional contacts, contrary to the claims of anti-diffusionist detractors. More than this, as will be shown later, the British diffusionists modified their theories over time and eventually began to add more complexity and nuance to their claims.

It is important to recognize that all three theorists were respected members of academia, working during a time in which they could not categorically be declared outsiders to anthropology. Two of the diffusionists, W. H. R. Rivers and Grafton Elliot Smith, were highly esteemed and widely-known professors who spent time at some of the most prestigious universities in the world such as Cambridge, Manchester, and University College, London. Together, Rivers and Elliot Smith are acknowledged as having made significant contributions to anatomy and physiology, neurology, psychiatry and psychology, ethnology, and paleoanthropology among others.

One problem that has emerged and needs to be addressed is that the historiography of ethnology/anthropology reflects a strong trend of present-mindedness and scientism as applied to previous theories. For example, the philological theories of missionary/ethnologist Robert Henry Codrington, along with his notions that civilization could have a negative impact on native peoples were dismissed in his own age. Codrington's proposition that cultural contact should be prevented when possible until a better assessment could be made of the consequences of such contact where ignored but, in a number of cases, it appears that he was correct on that issue and his warnings should have been heeded. This has been the case with British diffusionism as well. Generally, modern works on the history of anthropology approvingly trace the emergence and development of theories that are currently relevant or have attained broad acceptance. Concomitantly, the theories (such as Codrington's) that did not achieve such acceptance are criticized, downplayed, or rarely mentioned at all. This is particularly the case in textbooks that introduce new generations to the history of their discipline without any reference to the roles played by those who offered potentially constructive theories early on, yet were dismissed in their own time or slightly later due to a variety of circumstances that will be discussed herein.

    This work intends to demonstrate that British diffusionism was undermined very early on in relation to access to funds. When later scientific and archeological discoveries took place, the position of diffusionism within anthropology began further decline and fell under harsher criticism. For instance, several chronological errors emerged with the introduction of carbon-14 dating (C-14), which did not exist in the early years of the formulation of the diffusionist's theories. The diffusionists did, however, rely upon the best evidence available during their time and should not be criticized for what was only later to be discovered as chronological mistakes which were based upon the relative dating system of the time. However, in their attacks the subsequent histories often neglected a return to the abundant original source material and the actual claims made by the British diffusionists. In order to explicate the Heliolithic school of diffusion from its origins, it will be significant to begin by noting some of the key developments in each of their academic careers.

W. H. R. Rivers

The most widely known, and probably best remembered, member of the controversial diffusionists was William Halse Rivers Rivers (1864-1922). Trained in medicine and psychology, W. H. R. Rivers made numerous important contributions to psychotherapy, neurology, physiology, ethnology, and even folklore.[3] During his almost thirty year tenure (1893-1922) at Cambridge, Rivers worked diligently toward his goal of creating a rigorous methodology for ethnology.[4] Among the earliest results of this effort was his genealogical method, which grew out of Rivers' sensory perception field studies during the 1898 Torres Straits' Expedition and the 1901-1902 time spent amongst the Todas of southern India's Nigiri Hills.[5] Rivers believed he had found an important key for all of ethnology and anthropology in kinship studies through charting the relationships among every member of a society whom could answer his questions.

In his concern with kinship, Rivers was modifying the work of Lewis Henry Morgan (1818-1881). As Rivers wrote in an early report, "I began to collect the genealogies of the natives with the object of studying...the relationship to one another of the

---

[3] Henrika Kuklick, The Savage Within: The Social History of British Anthropology, 1885-1945, (New York: Cambridge University Press, 1992), 71.

[4] Richard Slobodin, W. H. R. Rivers, (New York: Columbia University Press, 1978), 15. Cambridge did not establish a professorship in anthropology until 1932; however, lectureships had been ongoing since the late 1800s.

[5] James Urry, Before Social Anthropology: Essays on the History of British Anthropology, (Reading: Harwood Academic Publishers, 1993), 27-28. The term 'field studies' is here meant to be taken only very generally, as the periods of study were not of qualitative length nor conducted in native languages.

individuals on whom we were making psychological tests."⁶ During this period, Rivers developed his understanding of social anthropology in his depictions of the changes of non-Western societies in terms of the prevalent interpretive mode of unilinear (or unilineal) evolutionism. During this period, Rivers made large numbers of charts and graphs depicting genealogical relationships.

Both Rivers' evolutionism and the genealogical method were fully exemplified in his massive work *The Todas* (1906). During a period of transition in virtually all fields of academia, Rivers was a polymath much like his colleague G. E. Smith. Rivers' accomplishments allowed him tremendous academic freedom to advance experimental psychology, while helping to establish anthropology as a fully professionalized university-based endeavor. British social ethnology followed Rivers' work with the Todas, particularly his genealogical method that included detailed relationship surveys to be used to explain social structure, behavior, and social cohesion. Rivers decided that social conditions determined kinship terminology.⁷ Highly influenced by Rivers' genealogical studies, one of Rivers' early students, A. R. Radcliffe-Brown would later be one of the two main progenitors of the structural-functionalist paradigm that "won out" over evolutionism and diffusionism.

Rivers was a convinced biological evolutionist, but it should be noted that he eventually rejected evolutionism when applied to the development of human societies (social evolutionism). While at Cambridge, Rivers collaborated with Charles Darwin's son Horace Darwin (1851-1928) on minor projects.⁸ It was to be much the same

---

⁶ W. H. R. Rivers, " A genealogical method of collecting social and vital statistics," *Journal of the Anthropological Institute of Great Britain and Ireland*, XXX, (1900), 74-82 passim.

⁷ Slobodin, W. H. R. Rivers, 2.

with his colleague G. E. Smith in that both admired the work of Charles Darwin, yet disagreed with their social evolutionist contemporaries.

Very early on, there were some signs that Rivers was beginning to deviate from the unilinear evolutionist perspective to a diffusionist view of the processes of culture change.[9] When Rivers worked with the Todas in the early 1900s, he proposed that some practices observed among the Todas could not have been native to those lands and were in fact brought from outside. He stopped short of speculating about origins for these practices and merely stated that they were 'survivals' without any practical application as he witnessed them employed.[10] During his career, Rivers was responsible for training England's first generation of professional anthropologists, which was to have an impact on the emergence of an anthropological alternative to socio-cultural evolutionism. This alternative was in part shaped by Rivers and, in later years, another who studied his works, namely Bronislaw Malinowski.

To account for the shift from an evolutionist to a diffusionist position, a number of authors, such as historian of anthropology Adam Kuper, have represented Rivers' intellectual development by proclaiming a drastic distinction between early Rivers and later Rivers.[11] These authors often assert that Rivers' great change emerged during the World War I psychiatric studies period in

---

[8] Ibid., 18.

[9] Ibid., 50. This is in contrast to some of the recent representations that Rivers' diffusionism was little more than a bizarre aberration which scholars should brush over or ignore.

[10] W. H. R. Rivers, The Todas, (New York: Macmillan, 1906), 712-719.

[11] Neither Rivers' biographer Richard Slobodin, nor historian of anthropology George Stocking, Jr. have agreed with Kuper's assessment.

which he worked with soldiers charged as deserters and cowards by their military due to shell shock syndrome.¹² This period of crisis has served a convenient role for a few historians of anthropology, who have often used this phase as a critical turning point to dissociate early evolutionistic Rivers from later diffusionistic Rivers. Thus, this reflects a bias of attempting to claim Rivers as an 'acceptable' founding father of the discipline, yet downplaying his later role in the development of the controversial diffusionist position. Rivers' views, nonetheless, put him inevitably into conflict with some of his peers.

As a precursor to his later battles with anthropologists, Rivers' critical stance toward some of his contemporaries could be seen to have emerged by the late 1880s during his association with George Bernard Shaw. Rivers was fond of the time he spent conversing with Shaw and the association was to affect him for the rest of his life.¹³ Rivers also spent time studying in Germany between 1892 and 1893 at Jena and Heidelberg respectively. His first temporary position at Cambridge began in 1894, with a permanent lectureship assigned in 1897. By 1900, Rivers was elected as a Fellow of the Royal Anthropological Institute and Fellow of the Royal College of Physicians.¹⁴ In 1908, Rivers traveled to Melanesia to conduct studies that eventually resulted in

---

¹² Today 'shell shock' is generally considered an unfortunate misnomer, better-termed post-traumatic stress disorder (PTSD). In 1920, Rivers published his account of the wartime stress studies called *Instinct and the Unconscious*, which was followed by a posthumous publication of further summations in *Conflict and Dream*. Both of these studies should be seen in the light of the numerous times during his life that Rivers' had pointedly opposed the problems presented by specialization in academia.

¹³ Slobodin, W. H. R. Rivers, 10, 68.

¹⁴ Ibid, 19-23.

his immense, though generally ignored in the disciplinary memory, publication of *The History of Melanesian Society* (1914). Rivers was quite proud of this production, which explicitly demonstrated his transition to a diffusionary perspective—while retaining some elements of evolutionist assumption and the doctrine of survivals common to degenerationist theory.[15]

In terms of psychology, like some of his colleagues, Rivers favored interdisciplinary/multidisciplinary studies.[16] Having helped to found the British Psychological Society in 1901 and the *British Journal of Psychology* in 1904, Rivers tended to favor a broad-based view of psychological and integrated biological studies.[17] In fact, as Rivers was to be among the first to introduce Freudian psychoanalysis in Britain, he also attempted to expunge what he felt was the overly sexualized basis of the field while emphasizing the biologically based aspects.[18] Rivers chose Carl Jung's claims of the universality of symbolism for special derision.[19] Rivers believed

---

[15] The traditional degenerationism emerged from Christian-inspired theories regarding the perfect origins of humanity in the Garden of Eden and the subsequent Fall of Man, which lead to an increasingly deteriorated world and its inhabitants.

[16] An intestinal problem (or strangulated hernia) took Rivers' life unexpectedly in 1922, as he was about to stand for election to a governmental position in representation of University College London.

[17] W. H. R. Rivers, Kinship and Social Organization, (London: Athlone Press, 1968), 16-33 passim; Paul Whittle, "W. H. R. Rivers: A Founding Father Worth Remembering," *Science as Culture*, Department of Experimental Psychology, University of Cambridge, http://human-nature.com/science-as-culture/whittle.html.

[18] What Rivers specifically attacked in Freudian psychology was the 'libido theory'.

[19] Slobodin, W. H. R. Rivers, 75.

Jung's work relied on a number of baseless and unscientific concepts without any biological founding principle. This position held implications also for Rivers' views on the processes of culture change. As mentioned by Elliot Smith in *Human History*, this predisposition lead Rivers to search for historically based alternatives—most notably those of cultural contacts as the solution to the questions he had about similarities found in widely separated societies.

G. E. Smith

Born in New South Wales, Australia, Grafton Elliot Smith (1871-1937) came to be among the most outspoken opponents of the social evolutionist approach to cultural change (often described as cultural progress by proponents). During his academic career, along with his numerous books, he published some 426 academic articles and papers.[20] In these publications, G. E. Smith made significant contributions to neuroanatomy, paleontology, primate evolution, anthropology, physiology, and biology. Elliot Smith is sometimes misleadingly referred to as an Egyptologist.[21] This label is incorrect because it implies an interest in and knowledge of Egyptian prehistory and history for its own sake, yet for G. E. Smith this was not his primary concern—he was concerned with the founding of civilization and the processes of cultural change.

He developed his interest in civilization and Egypt while he studied medicine and anatomy at the University of Sydney and

---

[20] Raymond A. Dart, "The Evolution of Man," in A. P. Elkin and N. W. G. Macintosh, eds., Grafton Elliot Smith: The Man and His Work, (Portland, Oregon: International Scholarly Book Services, 1974), 31.

[21] One example of this may be found in Glyn Daniel's 150 Years of Archaeology (1975).

carried out further research while under scholarship at Cambridge.[22] In 1897, he was in charge of the Central Nervous System section of the *Journal of Anatomy and Physiology* and contributed to the *Transactions of the Linnaean Society of London*.[23] Following an interest in ancient animal remains dating back to his childhood and reading works by Thomas Henry Huxley, Elliot Smith began more in-depth investigations of paleontology by 1898.[24] It has been suggested that his early work is best categorized as neuro-morphology, to which Elliot Smith was contributing as early as 1894-1896.[25] All of this research was interpreted in the context of biological evolution, to which Elliot Smith had been led by the writings of T. H. Huxley and was deeply committed to an approach that revolutionized further comparative neuroanatomical studies.

While at Cambridge, Elliot Smith completed a number of studies left in limbo by the passing of T. H. Huxley. G. E. Smith came into possession of virtually all of Huxley's notes, incomplete writings, and numerous projects that had only just begun. One such project was the completion of a massive catalogue of brains at the Royal College of Surgeons and others from all over the British Isles. Subsequent to attaining a medical degree in 1892, Elliot Smith continued work in this area and was awarded a gold medal for his thesis, "The Anatomy and Histology of the Cerebrum of the Non-Placental Mammal" (1895). While on scholarship at Cambridge University, he received a further scholarship from the British

---

[22] Kuklick, The Savage Within, 311.

[23] Warren Royal Dawson, ed., Sir Grafton Elliot Smith: A Biographical Record by His Colleagues, (London: Jonathan Cape, 1938), 24.

[24] Ibid., 26.

[25] Ibid., 185.

Medical Association in 1898. In 1902, Elliot Smith published a compendium of his studies of brains carried out in the Museum of the Royal College of Surgeons.

Upon completing additional studies, his efforts eventuated in being offered the Chair in Anatomy at the Governmental School of Medicine in Cairo in July 1900, which he promptly accepted.[26] Elliot Smith remained at the university in Cairo until 1909, at which time he left for the Chair of Anatomy at the University of Manchester, where he studied thousands of preserved brains from archeological research at El-Amrah of Upper Egypt. This resulted in a more prestigious appointment in 1907 as the Anatomical Advisor of the Archeological Survey of Nubia—leading to acceptance as a Fellow of the Royal Society (1907). In 1912, he received a Royal Medal of the Royal Society and he published "The Catalogue of the Royal Mummies in the Cairo Museum".[27] Professor George Thane's retirement in 1919 from University College, London, precipitated a move by the university to offer Thane's position as Chair in Anatomy to Elliot Smith, which he proudly accepted.

Over time, Elliot Smith became widely recognized for revolutionizing the study and teaching of anatomy. He did this by offering new perspectives on surface anatomy, radiological anatomy, and clinicals. Moreover, the postwar political climate was such that the United States and Britain wished to bring their university systems into closer alignment. Significant roles in this were played by the Carnegie Institute and the Rockefeller Foundation, each of which made extraordinary donations to British universities.

---

[26] Ibid. He had mentioned an interest in Egyptian prehistory as early as 1896, which suggests he would be eager to get there and begin investigations.

[27] This project was necessitated as part of a wider survey carried out prior to the flooding of the area for the Aswan Dam.

University College, London came to benefit magnificently from these cash distributions—particularly the medical sections.

To point up an example, in early 1920, coincident with Elliot Smith's appointment at UCL, the Rockefeller Foundation made initial grants of £370,000 and £835,000.[28] G.E. Smith went on to design and install a radiography unit, a medical science library (Thane Library), and a professorship in the History of Medicine. Ultimately, this resulted in Elliot Smith sending on over twenty former students to professorial chairs. Among his surgery and anatomy students were: H. H. Wollard (1889-1939), Raymond Dart (1893-1988), and Solly Zuckerman (1904-1993), each of whom made major contributions to anthropology and the human sciences. Herbert Wollard published *Progress in Anatomy* and eventually replaced Elliot Smith at UCL. G. E. Smith's career at University College, London lasted until his retirement in 1937. Throughout his lifetime, G. E. Smith received accolades from all over Britain.[29]

W. J. Perry

The final member of the trio, and probably the most widely read among the non-academic public, was William James Perry (1887-1949). At one time, Perry had been a student of Rivers while attending Cambridge on a mathematics' scholarship. Perry is commonly referred to in the literature variously as a geographer, ethnologist/anthropologist, Egyptologist, and historian. Nevertheless, his official academic position was that of Reader in Cultural Anthropology.

---

[28] Translated to dollars and adjusted for inflation, the figures would be the equivalent of approximately $17.8 million and $40.1 million dollars respectively today. Another intriguing point to note is that UCL was both coed and secular, which was a first for a university in England.

[29] In fact, Elliot Smith was knighted in 1934.

While attending Cambridge to study mathematics on scholarship, Perry became enamored with anthropology after attending lectures given by A. C. Haddon and W. H. R. Rivers. In fact, Rivers had collaborated with Perry as early as 1910 and Rivers noted his help in compiling *The History of the Melanesian Society*. Perry's first publication came in a 1914 issue of *Anthropos* and he first supported diffusionism in a paper at delivered to the 1915 British Association gathering.[30] His earliest impactful work was published as *The Megalithic Culture of Indonesia* (1918). Among Perry's other notable diffusionist publications were: *The Origin of Magic and Religion* (1923), *Social Organization, The Growth of Civilisation* (1924), *Gods and Men* (1927), and *The Primordial Ocean* (1935).

    A key differentiation between Perry and his diffusionist mentors Rivers and Elliot Smith was that, "Perry did not come to ethnology from a field of scientific endeavor to which he had already made significant and widely-acknowledged contributions."[31] As Reader in Comparative Religion from 1919 to 1923 at the University of Manchester, Perry produced some of his most important texts exemplifying his tremendous range of research interests. He was then offered the Upton Lectureship in the History of Religions at Manchester College, Oxford, which Perry accepted and retained from 1924 to 1927. From there, Perry moved to G. E. Smith's University College, London to accept the aforementioned position of Reader in Cultural Anthropology.[32]

---

[30] Ian Langham, <u>The Building of British Social Anthropology: W. H. R. Rivers and His Cambridge Disciples in the Development of Kinship Studies, 1898-1931</u>, (Boston: D. Reidel, 1981), 153.

[31] Ibid., 155.

[32] Perry stayed at UCL from 1928 until retirement in 1948.

Perry incorporated elements of Rivers' concepts about kinship studies and an array of other notions contained in the works of L. H. Morgan and Herbert Spencer (1820-1903).[33] However, Rivers' genealogical method was more analytical than the scant presentations proffered by either Morgan or Spencer, which led him to provide a more detailed and nuanced view of social development. This view acknowledged not only progress but fits and starts that either led nowhere or changes that were lost completely by the society in question. This ultimately led Perry, just as with Rivers, into theoretical conflict with the assumptions of unilinear social evolutionism.[34] Moreover, Perry abjured Freudian psychology as had Rivers.[35]

In 1926, Perry ascended to the leadership council of the Royal Anthropological Institute.[36] Some of Perry's students went on to play an important role in the development of anthropological theory. Anthropologist Adolphus Peter Elkin (1891-1979) was inspired by his UCL contacts with W. J. Perry to take up his studies and in 1934 took a position with the University of Sydney.[37] A. P. Elkin had thus returned to the site of the beginning of G. E. Smith's education. Another UCL product, Edwin Oliver James (1888-

---

[33] These elements were mainly terminology used by Morgan and Spencer to categorize behavior and societal traits.

[34] Social evolutionism is often equated with social Darwinism, though some recent studies have attempted to distinguish the two.

[35] W. J. Perry, Gods and Men: The Attainment of Immortality, (New York: William Morrow and Company, 1929), 83.

[36] Kuklick, The Savage Within, 63.

[37] A. P. Elkin, "Sir Grafton Elliot Smith: The Man and His Work—A Personal Testimony," in Elkin and Macintosh, eds., Grafton Elliot Smith: The Man and His Work, 11.

1972), later wrote *The Ancient Gods: The History and Diffusion of Religion in the Ancient Near East and the eastern Mediterranean* (1960).

  In sum, British diffusionism emerged in a period of academic transition and, as will be argued, met its demise through a loss of funding that enhanced the position of a younger generation of anthropologists. This factor, combined with the passing of the three British diffusionists, the radiocarbon revolution, and possibly most importantly, the failure of recent histories of the discipline to return to the primary sources, has led many anthropologists away from any realization of the beneficial role played by Heliolithic diffusionism in determining some of the key developments within British social anthropology and cultural anthropology as a whole. It is in this context, that it is important to realize that diffusionism did not emerge from a theoretical vacuum nor from any brand of extremism, rather, as will be shown, anthropological thought as well as a number of other fields of study had long embraced theories of diffusion very similar to that of the British diffusionists. These precursor theories, in fact, laid significant groundwork which allowed for the further development of an Egyptocentric diffusion scenario.

CHAPTER TWO

THEORETICAL CONTEXT

During the pre-World War I period, human behavior was understood to be explained through historical models—this was true for social evolutionists as well as diffusionists.[38] Social evolutionism (which, in general, proposed linear developmental stages of Savagery, Barbarism, and Civilization) is often considered the first paradigm of modern anthropology. The various applications of evolution that grew out of the works of Alfred Russel Wallace (1823-1913), Charles Darwin (1809-1882), and Jean-Baptiste Lamarck (1744-1829) were to range widely. In these visions, however, Victorian England was ensconced as the theoretical peak of social evolution up until that time along with all of the attendant implied moral valuations of persons and "races". All other societies were judged against this universalistic standard. Social evolutionist views very closely resembled the arguments used by social Darwinists at that time, who believed that all worthwhile progressive change in the human past resulted from conflicts with the stronger necessarily prevailing over the weaker. In other words, progress stemmed directly from violence. Though modern social evolutionists do not subscribe to such notions, it is difficult for them to convincingly argue that the presuppositions and arguments actually made by the earliest social Darwinists regarding concepts of superiority and purity never actually happened. Furthermore, these concepts were very popular among the socio-economic elite who

---

[38] Henrika Kuklick, The Savage Within: The Social History of British Anthropology, 1885-1945, (New York: Cambridge University Press, 1992), 75. Social evolutionism, in the sense here used, bears no relation with biological evolutionism and is not meant to imply any criticism of the biological version.

often combined their social Darwinism with concepts of "racial purification", fears of "miscegenation", and open approval of eugenicist policies on both sides of the Atlantic.

The carnage of World War I (1914-1918) drew much of Europe to a critical state of awareness as to the inadequacies of their conceptualizations of modern civilization. Thus, the war disabused many Victorians of their assumptions that their culture represented the pinnacle in social evolution. This sent many in academia and the public in search of alternative approaches to social anthropology, which had until then been quite satisfied with overly-simplistic representations of the 'ages and stages' (hunters to pastoralists to agriculturalists to civilization view) or the 'simple to complex' approach. These views were components of the cult of progress common during the time which sometimes tended toward a highly imaginative utopianism.

The implicit and explicit cult of progress faced a terrific dilemma. For example, evolutionists previously presented a "steady and gradual development, the expression of an inexorable progressive direction in history that was impeded only by irrational resistance to the inevitable."[39] In contrast, diffusionists found "an episodic past—periods of stasis intermittently punctuated by moments of drastic change."[40] Though, at times, both views were compatible with a few evolutionists, their views did not exist without resistance.

Among many in the wider public, there was a groundswell of popular opposition to anything that resembled Darwinian evolutionary theory. In fact, much of the public perceived an anti-Christian and generally anti-religious stance on behalf of academic social evolutionists. This was not entirely owed to biased

---

[39] Ibid.

[40] Ibid.

perception, as some social theorists were openly either agnostics or self-proclaimed "free-thinkers" which were anathema to proselytizers.[41] The social evolutionist perspective of a steady, almost teleological and progressivist form of social advancement conflicted with traditional Christian degenerationist views.[42] Though they would have been mistaken to some extent, perhaps some of the public perceived an ally in the Heliolithic diffusionist opposition.

The social evolutionist model was also made to serve colonial interests, as the theory implicitly justified powerful imperial positions in a "self-congratulatory" schema.[43] Evolutionists imposed a generally optimistic viewpoint on the future, as befitted their position as "members of the middle class, major beneficiaries of recent social trends."[44] This pattern was reinforced by biological and social museum displays radiating all over England and was, in turn, commended by both political Liberal and Conservative party members alike.[45] Major changes emerged as New Liberalism grew with its assumptions of collectivism and the subordination of individual rights to the so-called common good.[46] Eugenicist evolutionist anthropologists proclaimed individualism akin to 'primitive barbarism' thus rendering it, in their view, detrimental to

---

[41] Ibid., 78-79.

[42] Ibid., 81. This is a view of initial perfection from which humanity fell and much of human history since is considered to be a decline from that state (the Garden of Eden or Golden Age theory).

[43] Ibid., 93, 96.

[44] Ibid., 95.

[45] Ibid., 109.

[46] Ibid., 112.

social advancement.⁴⁷ Progress, however, remained in this vision as an inevitable process on the whole but not necessary for any specific society.⁴⁸

Diffusionism before the Heliolithic School

Along with the social evolutionist context, it is important to understand the relationship between that theory and anthropologist's use of diffusion as an explanatory scheme. Diffusion has a very long history dating to Greek and other Classical writings by Aristotle (382-322 BCE), Herodotus (484-432 BCE), Plato (427-347 BCE), Pliny (23-79 CE), and a plethora of others. These authors often wrote of connections between distantly separated peoples, massive migrations, and cultural interchange. In this context, it is important to note the extensive relationship between theories of diffusion and theories regarding the origins of civilization.⁴⁹

Many early diffusionist theories were based upon linguistics and preceded actual archeological work, but both fields of study were eminently concerned with the emergence of civilization and the question of origins in terms of languages, nations, and races. Several theorists postulated eastern or Asiatic origins for western civilization. For example, there was the German Jesuit polymath Athanasius Kircher (1601/2-1680) who proposed that Greece was not the originator of Western knowledge—rather it was to be located in ancient Egypt. In addition, in 1760, the Egyptian origin

---

⁴⁷ Ibid., 113.

⁴⁸ Ibid., 117.

⁴⁹ Martin Bernal, Black Athena: The Afroasiatic Roots of Classical Civilization, (New Brunswick, New Jersey: Rutgers University Press, 1991), v. II, 21, 64-74, 107-118, 187-300, 643-644, and passim.

for Chinese civilization was proposed by Joseph de Guignes (1721-1800). De Guignes, a French Orientalist, came to this notion through his study of Eastern languages, which led him to believe that Egyptians had actually colonized China.[50]

Similar notions about a widely spread Egyptian empire were espoused by William Stukeley (1687-1765). Although Stukeley, for his time, provided respectable archeological work on Avebury and Stonehenge (the results of these studies were published between 1740 and 1743), he also engaged in speculation regarding connections between the Druids, Stonehenge, and ancient Egyptians. This is another piece of evidence that demonstrates that the British diffusionists were not simply creating radical new views.[51]

In addition, James Cowles Prichard (1786-1849), who studied at Cambridge and Oxford, advanced a diffusion theory derived from philologically based ethnology and historical linguistics before the 1860s.[52] Prichard published *Analysis of the Egyptian Mythology* (1819), which attempted to bring ancient Egyptian records in line with biblical texts. In this and subsequent works, Prichard traced all peoples back to a single source—thus, he believed, proving the biblical texts historically accurate.[53] However, Prichard's main objective was to combat the polygenist heresy, which proposed multiple creations or multiple origins of humans and accounted for the observed global populational diversity in this

---

[50] Ibid.

[51] Ibid., 187-300 passim.

[52] George W. Stocking, Jr., After Tylor: British Social Anthropology, 1888-1951, (Madison: University of Wisconsin Press, 1999), 30.

[53] George W. Stocking, Jr., Victorian Anthropology, (New York: The Free Press, 1991), 48-53.

way. Therefore, Prichard attempted to establish human unity of the species and did so through a diffusionist argument.

Babylon Thesis

Albert Terrien de Lacouperie (1845-1895) was responsible for proposing a theory of the Mesopotamian origin for Chinese civilization. Lacouperie's 'Babylon thesis' was accepted by few Chinese, who were experiencing a periodic rise in nationalism that caused many to oppose external origin theories—or theories of diffusion into China.[54] By extension, many of these Chinese scholars also rejected diffusionists who posited Central Asian, Egyptian, or Indian origins.[55] Lacouperie, particularly in his *The Western Origins of Chinese Civilization* (1894), based his theories on grammatical and philological studies of 'pre-Chinese' languages. Though Lacouperie was no longer living, others in the West promoted the 'Babylon thesis' principally into the 1920s.[56] An important work in support of diffusion was C. J. Ball's *Chinese and Sumerian* (1913), which was soon countered by John Ross's *The Origins of the Chinese People* (1916) offering a more standard guise for anthropology.

In contrast to the supporters of Egyptian diffusionist claims, Hugo Winckler (1863-1913) supported yet another pan-Babylonian diffusionist theory. Winckler, an Assyriologist and professor at the University of Berlin, added a new impetus for diffusion in his 1892 *Geschichte Babyloniens und Assyriens*. Winckler derived multiple

---

[54] A.P. Elkin, "Grafton Elliot Smith and the Diffusion of Culture," A. P. Elkin and N. W. G. Macintosh, eds., Grafton Elliot Smith: The Man and His Work, (Portland, Oregon: International Scholarly Book Services, 1974), 202.

[55] Ibid.

[56] Ibid., 203.

connections through his philological studies and leapt to a number of questionable conclusions. These researches led to a flurry of publications supporting Mesopotamia-oriented diffusion theories which had been ongoing from about the 1850s through the 1910s. In fact, several books written by archeologists and Assyriologists were published on these topics through to the late 1930s.[57]

Another, somewhat distinct, school of diffusionists emerged from speculations regarding a root tongue (or the search for a mother language) proposed by the 18th century philologists. Importantly, social anthropologist Alan Barnard has claimed that, "Diffusionism had originated in the eighteenth-century philological tradition which posited historical connections between all languages of the Indo-European language family."[58] This would include the philologically oriented studies of William Jones (1746-1794), a British jurist and Orientalist, who began relevant linguistic-diffusion oriented publication in 1786-1787.[59] Jones noted similarities between Greek, Latin, and Sanskrit. This led him to propose a diffusion of peoples through what came to be known as the Indo-European protolanguage hypothesis.[60] These linguistic assumptions transferred easily into physical anthropology, which at the time viewed human racial groups in static terms that could easily

---

[57] Anne-Marie de Waal Malefijt, The Images of Man, (New York: Alfred A. Knopf, 1974), 162.

[58] Alan J. Barnard, History and Theory in Anthropology, (New York: Cambridge University Press, 2000), 47. Among the early terms for this speculative linguistic group (around the 1820s) were Indo-Germanic, Indo-Aryan, which were roughly equivalent to the modern term Indo-European.

[59] Ibid., 47.; Richard Poe, Black Spark, White Fire: Did African Explorers Civilize Ancient Europe?, (Rocklin, California: Prima Publishing, 1997), 358.

[60] Barnard, History and Theory, 47-48.

conjecture that there were direct connections between a people's language, their geographical origins, and phenotype (observed physical morphology). Here it is important to keep in mind that Jones' linguistic theory was yet another model for diffusionist argument that suggested to the British diffusionists the possibility of widespread human contacts.

Similar notions run like a stream through the works of Karl Wilhelm von Humboldt (1767-1835), Johann Gottfried von Herder (1744-1803), Jacob Grimm (1785-1863), and Franz Bopp (1791-1867). Most of these works were comparative studies of Indo-European grammars.[61] The Anglo-German Orientalist Friedrich Max Muller (1823-1900) carried out philological studies, mainly while at Oxford, that led him to similar claims. Specifically, Muller believed the origins of European languages could be found through researching Sanskrit sources and, unlike British diffusionism, much of this theory has tended to be more favorably reviewed by modern scholars.[62]

Among the remnants of these earlier forms of diffusionism, was the notion of 'culture-areas', exemplified in the work of Franz Boas and the students who he instructed and in Julian Steward's evolutionism.[63] Franz Boas began, in 1888, to take issue with speculative endeavors in ethnology and anthropology and, importantly, had worked under Adolph Bastian for a time at the Berlin Ethnographic Museum.[64] Moreover, Boas applied a

---

[61] Ibid., 48.

[62] Malefijt, The Images of Man, 161. It has even been speculated that German Romanticism began after Herder read some of the work of William Jones.

[63] Barnard, History and Theory, 47.

diffusionist approach to the theme of myths and their geographic spreading amongst societies.[65] Historian of archeology Bruce Trigger has suggested that an increased dependence on diffusionism was apparent in the publications of German ethnologist Friedrich Ratzel (1844-1901). Ratzel, who was also a geographer, adamantly disagreed with Adolph Bastian's notion of "psychic unity". In *Anthropogeographie* (1882-1891) and *The History of Mankind* (1896-1898), Ratzel asserted that ethnologists should be wary of claiming that complex inventions could routinely be repeatedly independently invented.[66] Here it should be pointed out that the concept of independent invention is often embraced as the direct counter of culture diffusionism, however, this may be a bit of a false division.

Anthropologist Edward Burnett Tylor (1832-1917) praised a number of Friedrich Ratzel's works.[67] One in particular was Ratzel's *Volkerkunde* (*The History of Mankind*). In relation to this, German-Austrian diffusionism was evident in the works of late nineteenth century geographer-anthropologists.[68] Bernhard Ankermann (1859-1943), who worked along with Fritz Graebner (1877-1934), helped develop what was termed the *kulturkreis* or culture-historical method, which remained in use mainly within ethnology. Ankermann studied the geographical diffusion of

---

[64] Stocking, After Tylor, 11. The importance of Bastian will be discussed at length later.

[65] Ibid., 11-30 passim.

[66] Bruce Trigger, A History of Archaeological Thought, (Cambridge: Cambridge University Press, 1990), 151.

[67] E. B. Tylor (1832-1917) was an early Oxford anthropologist who contributed to comparative studies of religion.

[68] Barnard, History and Theory, 49.

culture trait clusters and, together with Graebner, they were members of what is sometimes referred to as the Vienna school of ethnology. Austro-German culture-circle, culture cluster, or culture-area diffusionism was developed by Fritz Graebner, Wilhelm Schmidt, Schmidt's student Wilhelm Koppers (1886-1961), and, later, Friedrich Ratzel's student Leo Frobenius (1873-1938).

Leo Frobenius, who combined Bastian's approach of psychic unity and geographical diffusionism, like the Heliolithic school, researched solar mythologies. Frobenius did so in order to locate the migration patterns of the peoples of Oceanic regions. The British group of diffusionists, however, had little sympathy for the approach of Frobenius and his fellow German researchers and did not attempt to unify the German and British schools of diffusion.

In retrospect, the lack of a unification of the groups of British and German diffusionists was a tactical failure on the part of each group.[69] Elliot Smith noted that Frobenius's views were tainted with a tacit acceptance of Bastian's 'elementary ideas' and psychic unity concepts which were so anathema to his own. Frobenius also heavily drew upon the work of Friedrich Ratzel and incorporated Ratzel's concepts into his own about culture change; for example, Ratzel's critique of the anti-Darwinist elements in Bastian's theory of innate potential were to be of great influence in his scholarship.[70] Frobenius noted that Bastian's theories entailed the implication of universalized evolutionary stages that all cultures

---

[69] If the two groups had been willing to forge an alliance, the diffusionist approach may have lasted longer than it did. Thus, their lack of vision may be termed a tactical failure because they were not thinking about winning the academic dispute together.

[70] DeWitt Clinton Durham, "Leo Frobenius and the Reorientation of German Ethnology, 1890-1930" (Ph.D. diss., Stanford University, 1985), 97.

must pass through—akin to the scales previously mentioned of the social evolutionists.[71]

Frobenius and Elliot Smith agreed that Bastian's concept of innate ideas was unscientific.[72] They also held similar views on the significance of Darwin. Frobenius went so far as to attempt to incorporate the biological theory into his own ethnological theory. Frobenius's assistant Fritz Graebner elaborated these views.[73] Finally, Frobenius went on to develop what he called the 'evolutionary historical method' as an approach to culture, to which he adapted his personal distaste with modernity.[74]

In many ways, Elliot Smith and Perry came to share an antipathy toward modernity much like Frobenius and others in post-war Germany. They, however, differed on solutions to the perceived problems. Frobenius and others in Germany proposed an escape into intuition and a realization of the 'inner logic' of their home culture. On the other hand, Elliot Smith proposed an intellectual distancing from the ills of modernity in order to view this in the light of ancient civilizations wherein he believed that one could find corrections for some of the ills that he witnessed in his own era. In a similar context, Agnes Winifred Hoernle, who studied at Cambridge with A. C. Haddon and W.H.R. Rivers, also invoked diffusionist themes. These themes appeared in the U. S. in the 'culture area' and 'age area' hypothesis approach of Alfred Kroeber, Clark Wissler (1870-1947), and Melville Herskovits (1895-1963).[75]

---

[71] Ibid. This included an assumed uniformity of cultural evolution.

[72] Ibid., 100.

[73] Ibid., 111-112.

[74] Ibid.

[75] Stocking, After Tylor, 287-309.

Although these themes were shared by academics on both sides of the Atlantic, many histories of this period are tainted with an apprehension about the emergence of anti-modernism in the publications of academics. When linked with a supposed enthusiasm for "irrationalism" in other cultures, a few historians have associated this anti-modernism with the rise of National Socialism in Germany. Thus, anti-modernist views are often portrayed as only worthy of contempt, which included any beliefs that suggested pre-modern societies were more coherently organized (or integrated for peace) than modernist versions.[76] Due to these baseless attacks and fallacious reasoning, such views have compounded the opposition to diffusionism in recent times by conflating the concept with other disreputable views.

Egyptomania and the Heliolithic School

In the late 1700s, despite the efforts of Kircher and Stukeley, little was known about Egypt other than the scant information that could be gleaned from the Bible and early Greek and Roman sources.[77] It was not until the 1798-1799 invasion of Egypt by Napoleon Bonaparte (1769-1821) that a few European scholars could begin even cursory examinations.[78] Speculation about the race of the Egyptians was rampant following the Napoleonic invasion.[79] Two results of the studies carried out during this expedition were the multi-volume publication of the

---

[76] Durham, Leo Frobenius, 158.

[77] Trigger, A History of Archaeological Thought, 39.

[78] Ibid.

[79] Howard L. Malchow, Gothic Images of Race in 19th Century Britain, (Stanford, California: Stanford University Press, 1996), 18, 263.

Description de l'Egypte (1809-1828) and Jean-Francois Champollion's (1790-1832) decipherment of the Rosetta stone.[80] Another significant early scholar of Egypt was Karl Richard Lepsius (1810-1884). The Prussian archeologist Lepsius is widely recognized as one of the founders of modern Egyptology. In fact, due to the influence of these scholars, Egyptology was closely modeled on Classical studies, relying primarily upon written data for periodization, rulers and their reigns, values, and beliefs.[81]

By the late nineteenth century, Europeans and Americans were experiencing short periods of intense fascination with all things Egyptian.[82] This period of Egyptomania was in part inspired by Amelia Edwards' *A Thousand Miles up the Nile* (1876) and work by E.A.W. Budge (1857-1934) which was paid for by the Egypt Exploration Fund (1882).[83] As cultural historian Carl Schorske wrote on the topic of Egyptomania in *Thinking with History*, as early as the Renaissance period Europeans sporadically became enamored with Egypt's past. Schorske asserted that beginning with the work of philologists then, later, with the discoveries of archeologists, "the educated public" was dazzled by work being done in Egypt and followed the research intently and with great emotion.[84]

Archeologist Glyn Daniel (1914-1986) wrote that, "Up to 1900 the British, at first through the Egypt Exploration Fund, and later through Petrie's Egyptian Research Account...had a monopoly

---

[80] Trigger, A History of Archaeological Thought, 39.

[81] Ibid., 40.

[82] This is often referred to as Egyptomania.

[83] The Fund was later named Egypt Exploration Society

[84] Carl Schorske, Thinking with History: Explorations in the Passage to Modernism, (Princeton: Princeton University Press, 1998), 205.

of archaeological work in Egypt."[85] Moreover, many in England lauded imperialist practices, particularly following their 1882 entrance of Egypt, which marked the beginning of the so-called Scramble for Africa wherein European powers carved up Africa for occupation and the appropriation of natural resources to disastrous effect.[86] Finally, in 1921, the Egyptian Exploration Society entered the fray and brought with it a new fervor in the investigations of anything related to Egypt.[87]

In recent times, there have been a number of historians commenting on these periods of fascination with Egypt. Frequently, this historical commentary has attempted to minimize, discredit, and marginalize rival theories. More often, those opposed to a diffusionist perspective proclaim that Europe's interest in Egypt may safely be attributed to some mere amalgam of psychological motivations rather than actually searching for any real historical possibility of an ancient connection between the two regions. In explanation, social anthropologist Adam Kuper has written, "Diffusionism was given great impetus in Britain by the dramatic discoveries of Egyptian archaeology, and the development of the theory that the 'fertile crescent' was the cradle of most of the artifices of civilization."[88]

---

[85] Glyn Daniel, 150 Years of Archaeology, (Cambridge, Massachusetts: Harvard University Press, 1976), 195. France was also heavily involved in many of these endeavors.

[86] George W. Stocking, Jr., ed., Functionalism Historicized: Essays on British Social Anthropology, (Madison, Wisconsin: University of Wisconsin Press, 1984), v. II, 59.

[87] Daniel, 150 Years of Archaeology, 196.

[88] Adam Kuper, Anthropologists and Anthropology: The British School 1922-1972, (New York: Routledge, 1996), 15.

These periods of Egyptomania may have influenced both Rivers and G.E. Smith. Elliot Smith's attention moved to diffusion when in Egypt and perhaps before, however it is difficult to support such an assertion. As for Rivers, historian of science Ian Langham (1942-1984) wrote that, "It was while he was engaged in writing up the results of his 1908 expedition to Melanesia, that Rivers first became convinced of the crucial importance of diffusion in the development of human culture."[89] Rivers' 1908 Melanesian studies led to his publicly announced 1911 conversion to diffusionism from social evolutionism, as anthropologist and historian of anthropology George Stocking, Jr. wrote on this topic, "Before one could attempt to find general laws of evolutionary development, there must be an historical analysis 'of the cultures…now spread over the earth.'"[90] In his 1906 work on the Todas, the final chapter focused on the ethno-historical method with a diffusionary approach—this effort was a precursor to the later theories of the Heliolithic approach to culture.[91]

---

[89] Ian Langham, The Building of British Social Anthropology: W. H. R. Rivers and His Cambridge Disciples in the Development of Kinship Studies, 1898-1931, (Boston: D. Reidel, 1981), 118.

[90] Stocking, Victorian Anthropology, 321.

[91] Stocking, "Radcliffe-Brown and British Social Anthropology," in Functionalism Historicized, 141-142.

The Lineage of Diffusionism in England and Continental Europe: *Ex Oriente Lux* and Egypt[92]

Both sides in the interpretive conflict, *Le Mirage Oriental* and *Ex Oriente Lux*, were diffusionary schools of thought that merely proposed differing centers of culture dispersal. In 1912, Flinders Petrie in his *Revolutions of Civilization* wrote about the importance of human migration and the attendant cultural and biological changes in peoples that resulted.[93] This appeared to parallel a diffusionist outline, though Petrie did not apply it extensively enough to draw the ire of his fellow Egyptologists or recent histories of anthropology.[94] Petrie's book was later followed by Harold Peake and H. J. Fleure's *The Corridors of Time* (1927), which proposed a diffusion scheme similar to that of archeologist/philologist Vere Gordon Childe (1892-1957) regarding population movements from the Mediterranean regions into parts of Europe.[95]

Diffusionism is also clear in the archeological work of the Swedish scholar Oscar Montelius (1843-1921).[96] At least, this

---

[92] J. Peter White, "Early Man in New Guinea," in Elkin and Macintosh, eds., Grafton Elliot Smith, 109-113.

[93] Ibid., 238. *Le Mirage Oriental* was described by Louis Bertrand (1866-1941) in his book by the same name published in 1910, as intended to oppose the then prevalent *Ex Oriente Lux*, which proposed that many of the attainments of European society had been introduced from the outside, specifically from Asiatic sources.

[94] Elkin, "Elliot Smith and the Diffusion of Culture," in Elkin and Macintosh, eds., Grafton Elliot Smith, 152.

[95] Daniel, 150 Years of Archaeology, 248.

[96] Barnard, History and Theory, 52.

applies to the theories that Montelius constructed to explain certain discoveries. Archeology historian Bruce Trigger has commented that Montelius constructed a chronological outline that attempted to demonstrate the high cultural accomplishments of the Near East, which radiated outward to Europe. This meant that Europe "was for long but the pale reflection of Eastern civilization" and, according to Trigger, that Montelius was to be the "most distinguished exponent of a diffusionist explanation of European cultural development" being of the *Ex Oriente Lux* school.[97]

Oscar Montelius formulated an archeological theory of diffusion that was prevalent for a significant period. Montelius linked the origins of European civilization with movements emanating from the ancient Near East. The *Ex Oriente Lux* ('Light from the East') group of diffusionists also included John Myres (1869-1954), and the Australian V. Gordon Childe. Others, such as H. J. Massingham (1888-1952), entertained the notion of diffusions from the Near East into England in the ancient past which left indelible impacts on the people for centuries.

It is perhaps the later associations some have attempted to make between the Aryanist diffusion theories of Gustav Kossina (1858-1931), which have made impossible any recent consideration of the Heliolithic approach. Unfortunately, Himmler and other Nazis took the works of Kossina as "scientific" support for their racialist theories which were rooted in hate, a false belief in "racial purity", and ethnic discrimination. Historians of science subsequent to the Second World War have tended to lump together all similar anthropological grand theorizing, particularly those in a diffusionist mode, with the likes of Kossina as potentially dangerous and possibly racist. However, the Heliolithic school never subscribed to any notion of a migrating and conquering 'master

---

[97] Trigger, <u>A History of Archaeological Thought</u>, 159-160.

race', or racism of any sort. In fact, they tended to be very cosmopolitan and accepting of all of humanity in their worldview.[98]

Judged in the context of long European traditions of citing a key role for the Near East in general, and the Egyptian to Mesopotamian regions in specific, there was little in the arguments of the Heliolithic school that was unprecedented. The claims as to the school's extremism can only stand in strictly relativistic terms—that is to say that the diffusionists were only a point of contrast to their rival schools of thought (evolutionism and structural-functionalism) or current systems of anthropological thought. The British diffusionists were a part of an extensive European tradition of studies regarding the Near East among academics of the time.

The British diffusionist's concerns were not motivated by obsession, Egyptophilia, or Egyptomania, though they were perhaps influenced by these periodic societal flare-ups. Rather, they were interested in discovering the roots of civilization, the role played by the Neolithic revolution, and the origins of agriculture. Among professional Egyptologists, such as E.A. Wallis Budge (1857-1934) and William Matthew Flinders Petrie (1853-1942), diffusionism was of little issue because they were concerned with artifacts and localized histories of the people they were investigating. From 1894 to 1924, Budge served as Curator of Egyptian and Assyrian Antiquities at the British Museum and managed to remain above the fray in the debates over diffusionism in the 1920s. W.M.F. Petrie only employed diffusionist arguments in a closely limited sense and wrote principally on predynastic Egypt and dynastic political changes.[99]

In Germany and Austria from the 1880s to the 1930s, there emerged yet another influential school of anthropological diffusion

---

[98] Stocking, After Tylor, 218-401 passim.

[99] Ibid.

theory briefly mentioned earlier. Elaborated by Friedrich Ratzel, Wilhelm Schmidt (1868-1954), Robert Fritz Graebner, Wilhelm Koppers, and Leo Frobenius, the *kulturkreis* (culture-circle) version of diffusionist theory attained preeminence in continental Europe and, curiously, impacted some anthropologists in the Americas. These scholars were primarily geographers, ethnographers, and ethnologists. This group postulated several primary centers of diffusionary movements.

Though Elliot Smith was familiar with this school of diffusionism, he criticized their methods on various occasions. For many years, even in the United States, diffusionism played a role in anthropology and tended to be framed as a buttress against social evolutionism's unilinear model of progress and stages. Franz Boas (1858-1942) studied the spread of ideas and behaviors in North America among aboriginal Native Americans. Later, one of Boas' understudies, Alfred Kroeber (1876-1960) utilized a culture area approach to the spread of peoples which resembled Austro-German diffusionism. Kroeber took a decidedly historical approach to the development of cultures, rather than offering presentist functional explanations for trait distributions.[100]

In order to trace the distribution of traits, Rivers, Elliot Smith, and Perry each applied the concept of the doctrine of survivals in their studies. As in the writings of E. B. Tylor, they thought that elements of previous modes of living were retained in modern activities, however, without the same cultural meaning. Through this approach, the Heliolithic school believed they could discern past movements or connections between societies—and, from that, determine the source of origin using the 'comparative method'.[101] Finally, so that one may get to the root of their

---

[100] Ibid.

philosophy, it is also important to note the impetus of the diffusionist's early rival theories of independent invention and the role played by Adolph Bastian—who was roundly criticized by Elliot Smith. It is to this topic which we shall now turn our concern.

---

[101] Here, the comparative method is not meant to be confused with the current understanding and use of the term by anthropologists since the British diffusionists were more concerned with cultural similarities rather than contrasts.

CHAPTER THREE

ADOLPH BASTIAN: PSYCHIC UNITY

Adolph Bastian (1826-1905) is of profound importance in relation to the British diffusionists because he drew special ire in the works of G. E. Smith. Primarily, for Elliot Smith, this was due to the philosophical linkages between the assumption of psychic unity and social evolutionism. Elliot Smith promoted the notion of the uniqueness of civilization, which was rather at odds with the presumption of psychic unity as it implied the potential replication of the emergence of civilization any number of times. For Elliot Smith, there could be nothing more absurd because it violated the concept of the chance occurrence of civilization's initial emergence.

Bastian was among the founders of ethnography and ethnology. As a founder, he was responsible for the theoretical development of the notion of 'psychic unity'; he proposed a form of multilinear (or multilineal) social evolutionism in contradistinction to most of his contemporaries and he opposed polygenist views of human origins by instead supporting the monogenist concept of the unity of humankind.[102] Bastian based his theoretical developments on a solid background education from a number of fields of study.

To elaborate, Bastian studied medicine, jurisprudence, and the natural sciences at several German universities. He was a noted traveler who produced accounts of his voyages and contacts with non-Western peoples. Furthermore, Bastian helped found the

---

[102] In this context, polygenists were those who believed races should be viewed in a stationary physicalist sense. These races were considered to have been pre-adapted to specific climatic regions, whereas monogenists viewed races as products of a variety of movements through numerous environments to which they adapted over time. The Heliolithic diffusionists were also monogenists.

Berlin Society for Anthropology, Ethnology and Prehistory. It was in these arenas that Bastian was able to propound his many theories on humanity.[103]

Bastian believed that 'elementary ideas' (*elementargedanken*) and 'folk-ideas' (*volker-gedanken*) developed out of the universalized basis of psychic unity, which led to similar inventions in distant and entirely unconnected geographical regions. He explained the cultural variations observed as having been altered by the differing environments of the inventors. Bastian believed in a predetermined world or a predestined order of nature, governed by natural laws that may be rationally discovered.[104] And, in many ways, he owed an intellectual debt to Theodor Waitz (1821-1864) who made significant contributions to psychology in addition to anthropology.[105] Waitz, while professor of philosophy, began publication in 1859 of his six-volume masterwork on anthropology which was enthusiastically read by Bastian.[106]

Bastian was also significantly influenced by Isidore Auguste Marie François Xavier Comte (1798-1857) and his intellectual

---

[103] Klaus-Peter Koepping, <u>Adolph Bastian and the Psychic Unity of Mankind: The Foundations of Anthropology in Nineteenth Century Germany</u>, (St. Lucia: University of Queensland Press, 1985), 233, n. 5.; James Whitman, "From Philology to Anthropology in Mid-Nineteenth-Century Germany," in George W. Stocking, Jr., ed., <u>Functionalism Historicized: Essays on British Social Anthropology</u>, v. II, (Madison: University of Wisconsin Press, 1988), 224.

[104] Koepping, <u>Adolph Bastian and the Psychic Unity of Mankind,</u> 113.

[105] Ibid., 127.

[106] James Whitman, "From Philology to Anthropology in Mid-Nineteenth-Century Germany," in George W. Stocking, Jr., ed., <u>Functionalism Historicized</u>, 230. Waitz was an evolutionist who opposed polygenist interpretations of human origins.

predecessors.[107] The French philosopher Comte was, in turn, influenced by Marie Jean Antoine Nicolas de Caritat Condorcet (1743-1794) by way of Claude Henri de Rouvroy (Comte de Saint-Simon) (1760-1825). In Auguste Comte's *Course of Positive Philosophy* (1830-1842), it was postulated that knowledge developed through three levels—theological, metaphysical, and positive or, as stated elsewhere by Comte: deities, theoretic abstractions, and other phenomena.[108] Bastian also duplicated Auguste Comte's three-stage schema of mental development from the base "savage" that operates in a sensual-emotive or theological/religious realm, to the metaphysical, and finally to the scientific or positive.[109] In this, one can see the path by which social evolutionism could emerge and be grafted into ethnology and anthropology.

Based upon these elements, it may be concluded that both the Enlightenment and Romanticism influenced Bastian.[110] For instance, Bastian acknowledged his debt to the works of Johann Gottfried von Herder (1744-1803). Herder took a secular approach to biblical interpretation, which drew on the scholastic pursuit of what is known as higher biblical criticism that tended to undermine the religious orthodoxy of the time on several fronts. Herder's works also contained strong themes of egalitarianism and granted that ideas of a people may vary widely from period to period.

---

[107] Paul A. Erickson and Liam D. Murphy, <u>A History of Anthropological Theory</u>, (New York: Broadview Press, 2001), 38.

[108] Ibid., 38.

[109] Ibid., 96.

[110] Koepping, "Enlightenment and Romanticism in the work of Adolf Bastian: The historical roots of anthropology in nineteenth century," in Han F. Vermeulen and Arturo Alvarez Roldan, eds., <u>Fieldwork and Footnotes: Studies in the History of European Anthropology</u>, (London: Routledge, 1995), 76.

Herder, the Romantic, admonished all to 'judge each time and culture by its own canon of values'.[111] Bastian's notion of 'elementary thoughts' assumed social evolutionary convergence would result from those thoughts common to all humankind.[112] This can also be found in Herder's concept that language operates as a restricting mechanism which partially determines thought-worlds. However, there was still more to Bastian's scientific views.

In addition to the influence of positivism, Bastian was thoroughly rooted in Cartesian philosophy and the French Enlightenment in addition to the Romantic German counter-movement.[113] For the counter-movement, "Both human affairs and nature were believed to be governed by the same kind of laws."[114] In a determined world, such as that envisioned by Bastian, science views 'man as machine'. Auguste Comte and Emile Durkheim (each of whom according to Alan Barnard represents conservative elements of Enlightenment thought) advanced views on rules, property relations, and hierarchies of natural organization—then interpreted these into the social sciences.[115] This led to two outcomes: one, the use of the scientific method to study society and application of findings to "improve" society, and two, the notion that society is based upon hierarchy and the related socio-structural organization for survival. Bastian also found similar views in the

---

[111] Ibid., 78.

[112] Alan J. Barnard, <u>History and Theory in Anthropology</u>, (New York: Cambridge University Press, 2000), 49.

[113] Ibid., 80.

[114] Ibid.

[115] Barnard is professor of anthropology at the University of Edinburgh and specializes in the history of anthropology, particularly 18th century anthropological ideas.

writings of Voltaire and Condorcet which worked to amplify his own convictions.[116]

Bastian, in a surprising turn of thought, combined these views with the more radical theories of French political philosopher Jean-Jacques Rousseau (1712-1778) and Denis Diderot (1713-1784). Bastian thus believed that true equality could only be attained through education. One of Bastian's instructors, Friedrich Wilhelm Heinrich Alexander von Humboldt (1769-1859), connected him to the debate on diffusion-independent invention.[117] Though the British diffusionists were highly critical of his concept of psychic unity, Bastian never denied the role of diffusion in culture change—however, he did insist that in order to get to the most pristine of the so-called elementary ideas, one would require cultures to exist in geographical isolation.[118] Strikingly similar ideas were carried on by Bastian and numerous supporters even today whether they acknowledge his contributions or not.

It could even be said that Bastian and his followers were forging ahead in an attempt to create a science of humanity. Thus, "This hyper-scientific, anti-humanistic, and "positivist" attitude made the new cultural evolutionism and New Archaeology pills too bitter for many anthropologists to swallow."[119] Perry, Rivers, and Elliot Smith found these moves on behalf of Bastian's cohorts to be much too problematic. The British diffusionists remained humanists, in a classical sense, throughout their careers as opposed scientism and positivism altogether.

---

[116] Ibid., 81.

[117] Ibid., 81-82.

[118] Ibid., 85, 87.

[119] Erickson and Murphy, <u>A History of Anthropological Theory</u>, 121.

In further contrast, Bastian was also "a staunch opponent of Darwinism."[120] In fact, the rather zealous biological evolutionist and culture diffusionist Ernst Heinrich Philipp August Haeckel (1834-1919) attacked Bastian for his opposition to biological evolution.[121] In the minds of those such as Haeckel, Elliot Smith, and Perry, these notions all appeared to be directly linked. In fact, this meant that the diffusionists disagreed with almost everything espoused by their opposition—they saw claims of psychic unity, social evolutionism, and opposition to Darwinian biological evolution as intimately interconnected. Grafton Elliot Smith wrote about these issues by pointing to a countermovement and stating that renowned anthropologists Philip Meadows-Taylor, Henry Lane Fox Pitt-Rivers, James Fergusson, and James Park Harrison, "...were explaining the similarities that are found widespread throughout the world to the diffusion of features of culture from some original center where each of them was first invented."[122] Nonetheless, within a decade, several of Bastian's theories had become ascendant.

Elliot Smith saw this dominance tied to a number of other related developments. More specifically, Elliot Smith was discouraged by the impact of neo-Platonism and William Robertson's *History of the Americas* (1777).[123] His opposition to Robertson was due to the promotion of the 'Law of Nature' which Robertson claimed demonstrated that 'in similar circumstances any

---

[120] Barnard, History and Theory, 49.

[121] Grafton Elliot Smith, Conversion in Science, (Great Britain: Richard Clay and Sons, Limited, Bungay, Suffolk, 1929), 26. Haeckel was, however, also a polygenist and typological/racialist thinker.

[122] Ibid.

[123] Ibid., 22.

people could invent similar customs and beliefs'.[124] G. E. Smith believed this was too close to the independent invention/psychic unity principle of the similarity of the working of the human mind.[125] Elliot Smith thought this to be an absurd and unproven sentiment that was widely and uncritically accepted during his day and it was, in a sense, his mission to undermine this view.

G. E. Smith was highly disparaging of the work of German psychologist Wilhelm Maximilian Wundt (1832-1920) and, later, Swiss psychiatrist Carl Gustav Jung's (1875-1961) use of Bastian's concepts.[126] Moreover, Elliot Smith, much like W. J. Perry, saw Bastian's ethnological theory of psychic unity to be the equivalent of biology's spontaneous generation theory.[127] G. E. Smith wrote, "Nations do not flourish in watertight compartments. Diffusion of culture has been taking place throughout the whole history of civilization."[128] Nonetheless, the British diffusionists were criticized by Bastian's followers, who suggested that the diffusionists somehow insisted that humankind is utterly incapable of a vast array of individual inventiveness regardless of what they were actually writing and such attacks have continued to this day.

Due to this, it should be pointed out that Elliot Smith did not claim that humans were generally uninventive, but he did claim that there was no *need* for certain very specific creations of, what he

---

[124] Ibid.

[125] Ibid., 23.

[126] Grafton Elliot Smith, "A Note on 'The Aims of Ethnology'," in W. H. R. Rivers, Psychology and Politics: And Other Essays, (New York: Harcourt, Brace and Company, Inc., 1923), 144-145.

[127] Smith, Conversion in Science, 26.

[128] Grafton Elliot Smith, The Ancient Egyptians and the Origin of Civilization, (New York: Harper, 1923), 203.

considered to be, superficial artificialities. G. E. Smith did not mean that any group or culture was incapable of invention and, in fact, specifically because all were indeed perfectly capable, he believed, proved his point; there was no need for certain inventions to take place and thus no necessity for the emergence of civilization for thousands of years.[129] This, the diffusionists insisted, was but another of many disagreements between Bastian's views and their own.

    Finally, G. E. Smith believed that the food-gatherer band was the ultimate normative standard of judgment for the ethical and moral status of modern civilization—this was essentially the reverse of Bastian's arguments and many social evolutionists and social Darwinists who followed. The diffusionists suggested there was no tendency toward the acquisition or accumulation of objects beyond immediate, personal needs.[130] According to Elliot Smith, this included egalitarian redistribution of goods or sharing because, "The society in which all is peace is the healthy society...the type of behaviour in family groups is stable, happy, cheerful, and lacking in violence. This may...be regarded as the standard of behaviour for human society."[131] To expand upon these themes and take a more in-depth view of the diffusionists and their philosophical presuppositions, it may be helpful to analyze the works of and source material found in W. H. R. Rivers' publications.

---

[129] Grafton Elliot Smith, <u>Human History</u>, (New York: W. W. Norton and Company, Inc., 1929), 245.

[130] Ibid., 246.

[131] Ibid., 247.

CHAPTER FOUR

RIVERS' SOURCES

W. H. R. Rivers wrote *History and Ethnology*, to oppose the "crude evolutionary standpoint" by which he meant unilineal social evolutionism.[132] Rivers intended to demonstrate the extraordinary level of complexity of cultural change.[133] He believed there was a close affinity between his own work and that of legal historian Frederic William Maitland (1850-1906), particularly Maitland's "The Body Politic" (1875).[134] F. W. Maitland was a medieval law scholar at the University of Cambridge, who emphasized the importance of science and the procedures of science for historians.[135] Maitland included archeology within the field of history and thus sought broad applicability for scientific methodology and it was with this that Rivers agreed. Maitland was also very disturbed by social evolutionists 'filling in gaps of knowledge' without evidence and only generalization and supposition for earlier 'stages' of human existence.[136]

---

[132] W. H. R. Rivers, History and Ethnology, (London: The Macmillan Company, 1922), 3.

[133] Ibid., 5.

[134] Ibid., 29.

[135] Frederic William Maitland, "The Body Politic," in A Historical Sketch of Liberty and Equality, as Ideals of English Political Philosophy from the Time of Hobbes to the Time of Coleridge, (Indianapolis: Liberty Fund, 2000), 183-188.

[136] Ibid., 193-194.

In 1924, while at UCL, Elliot Smith penned a preface to W. H. R. Rivers' posthumously released work entitled *Medicine, Magic and Religion*. This 1924 publication was part of general editor C. K. Ogden's "International Library of Psychology, Philosophy and Scientific Method". This series contained such prominent contributors as Ludwig Wittgenstein, C. G. Jung, C. S. Pierce, Bertrand Russell, Paul Radin, Bronislaw Malinowski, and Edward Sapir; these volumes were to offer three works by Rivers—*Conflict and Dream*, *Psychology and Politics*, *Psychology and Ethnology*, and Grafton Elliot Smith's *The Psychology of Myths*. More than this, G.E. Smith added a 1919 John Rylands Library (Manchester) lecture presented by Rivers on *Mind and Medicine*, which reflected his increasingly diffusionist position.[137]

Rivers' diffusionism attempted to combine the "historical and evolutionary" approach in ethnology and anthropology.[138] He stated that independent development, as proposed by Adolph Bastian, was not false but "it is far from being the whole truth."[139] It is, however, never clear in *Medicine, Magic and Religion*, or any other work, that Rivers accepted the trait list method preferred by Perry and Elliot Smith. Nevertheless, Rivers analyzed a number of the world's continents for possible connections much like G. E. Smith and W. J. Perry.

Rivers compared the diffusion of civilization to England from Greeks, Arabs, French, Turks, and Russians to the rest of the world's attainments and discounted independent invention as the sole possibility because otherwise, "peoples who inhabit these continents and islands were somehow able to discover arts which

---

[137] W. H. R. Rivers, in G. E. Smith, ed., Medicine, Magic and Religion, (London: Kegan Paul, Trench, Trubner, Company Limited, 1924), vii.

[138] Ibid., 55-60.

[139] Ibid., 58.

we, who think ourselves so greatly their superiors, were content to learn from other peoples."[140]

In the Wake of Rivers

W. J. Perry, while studying mathematics in 1906 at Cambridge, became a close associate of Rivers around 1910-1911.[141] Rivers, in fact, had suggested aspects of Perry's later Heliolithic research program to him as early as 1913.[142] Perry was greatly impressed with the implications of diffusion and proceeded to fully investigate the possibility of widespread human cultural contacts.

In 1918, W. J. Perry published *The Megalithic Culture of Indonesia*, wherein he compiled the results of his earliest studies. Perry dedicated this book to W. H. R. Rivers—whom Perry said had frequently advised him during the research process and who had initially suggested that he specifically take on the topic the origin and spread of megalithic culture.[143] Prior to publication, Perry had G. E. Smith, A. C. Haddon, and A. M. Hocart read the manuscript version and offer their suggestions for changes.[144] The book was published due to G. E. Smith's efforts with the Manchester University Press, demonstrating an early professional

---

[140] Ibid., 85.

[141] George Stocking, Jr., After Tylor: British Social Anthropology, 1888-1951, (Madison, Wisconsin: University of Wisconsin Press, 1985), 214.

[142] Ibid.

[143] W. J. Perry, The Megalithic Culture of Indonesia, (London: Longman's, Green and Company, 1918), Publications of the University of Manchester, Ethnological Series No. III, vii-198, ix passim.

[144] Ibid., x.

connection between them.[145] In this work, Perry researched what he termed the Indonesian Megalithic Culture.[146] He called this a 'culture-mixture', by which he meant a dual organization of society very much akin to the structural notion promulgated by Rivers.

In *The Megalithic Culture of Indonesia*, Perry's geographical definition of Indonesia referred to: the East Indian Archipelago, Assam, Burma, the Malay Peninsula, the Philippine Islands, and Formosa.[147] Perry was reassured that his method was correct because Rivers had applied the 'culture-mixture' hypothesis successfully to Melanesia. Perry ranged too far, however, and constructed a number of dubious linguistic derivations, which diffusionism's detractors immediately noted.[148] As is apparent from the quotations and citing of evidence, Perry had, like Elliot Smith, relied on C. F. Oldham's diffusionist work *Serpent and the Sun* (1905) which discussed the long history of serpent and solar worship found in many ancient cultures around the world. Moreover, John Wilfrid Jackson's (1880-1978) *Shells as Evidence of the Migrations of Early Culture* (1917) was instructive for Perry and he, like G. Elliot Smith, cited evidence of culture diffusion from this book. These works provided a loose argumentative structure and demonstrated to other academics that the diffusionist approach had important antecedents, which recent histories of anthropology have tended to ignore in the zeal to denigrate the concept.

W. J. Perry also drew on the works of many other contemporary scholars for evidence beyond his own expertise. For example, in his *Gods and Men* (1929) Perry relied upon George

---

[145] Stocking, After Tylor, 214.

[146] Perry, The Megalithic Culture of Indonesia, vii-viii.

[147] Ibid., 1.

[148] Ibid., 87.

Amos Dorsey (1868-1931). G. A. Dorsey worked with Alfred Kroeber and was widely published on native North American mythologies such as that of the Arapaho, Cheyenne, Osage, Pawnee, and Wichita among others. Dorsey was Harvard's first doctoral graduate in anthropology and his colleague A. L. Kroeber, much like G. E. Smith, was a critic of the social evolutionist appeal to cultural 'autogenesis'.[149] Thus, when these works were brought together by Perry, they flowed harmoniously in theoretical agreement. From this it can be seen that Perry remained committed to the views of Rivers and Elliot Smith. All three diffusionists, even in their separate works, were consistent in the types of evidence that they cited.

Classicist and antiquarian Cecil Torr's (1857-1928) studies of the possible links between Egypt and Greece in the past (1271-850 BCE) were helpful to both W. J. Perry and Elliot Smith. Torr also wrote *Rhodes in Modern Times* (1887), which E. A. W. Budge often quoted. There was also the work of Francis de la Port Castelnau (1818-1880), who went on a number of expeditions to the Americas and published on geographical, entomological, botanical, and other scientific observations. This more fully demonstrates that not only the diffusionists, but also a number of their contemporary scholars cited similarly acceptable evidence though, admittedly, not in support of Heliolithic diffusionism. Yet, even more examples exist of contemporary academics who were writing to similar ends.

For example, Perry also used Julius Eggeling's translation of *The Satapatha-Brahmana* (1882-1900), which was part of a series

---

[149] A. P. Elkin, "Elliot Smith and the Diffusion of Culture", in A. P. Elkin and N. W. G. Macintosh, eds., Grafton Elliot Smith: The Man and His Work, (Portland, Oregon: International Scholarly Book Services, 1974), 146. They each noted the links between psychic unity, independent invention, and cultural autogenesis theories.

called 'The Sacred Books of the East'.[150] Eggeling worked on this series along with the noted diffusionist general editor F. Max Muller. In addition, Perry cited Samuel Henry Hooke (1874-1968) who wrote *New Year's Day* (1927), a key work on calendrical studies. Based upon Hooke's knowledge of Assyrian, Babylonian, and Middle Eastern mythology, Perry found this work on comparative religion and mythology reliable and suitable to a diffusionist interpretation.[151]

Perry also found diffusionist implications beyond mythology in more tangible areas of research, which included the studies by Maurice Gompertz on the origin of agriculture.[152] In *Corn from Egypt*, Gompertz asserted ancient dates for the beginnings of cultivation in Egypt, which very much resembled the claims found in a series of contemporary works such as: H. J. Massingham's *The Golden Age*, Irene J. Curnow's *Maps and Charts*, and British Classicist Charles Theodore Seltman's *Image and Superscription*. Perry's analysis of these works led him to some of his most important claims which included who he believed to be the original civilizing peoples.

Among Perry's substantive contentions, were that he had pinpointed the beginnings of what he called the 'Children of the Sun' around 2750 BCE during Egypt's Fifth Dynasty.[153] Perry noted the growth in intensity of the solar cult and the increased

---

[150] W. J. Perry, Gods and Men: The Attainment of Immortality, (New York: William Morrow and Company, 1929), 87.

[151] Ibid., 89.

[152] Ibid.

[153] Ibid., 40-55. Currently the Fifth Dynasty is dated roughly between 2465-2323 BCE.

importance of the Heliopolitan priesthood. Perry wrote, "At that time the kings began to use the name of the sun, Re, in their royal protocols; and the eighth king of that dynasty, Dedkere-Isisi, was the first man known to have called himself by the title Son of the Sun."[154] Based upon these discoveries, Perry went on to trace potential connections among sky and sun deities all over the world, which he believed emanated from this period in Egypt. For these assertions, Perry tended to rely upon local experts such as anthropologist A. P. Elkin's research in Australia.[155] Very little of this research appears to have been used by contemporary Egyptologists, but the emphasis on sun cults and megalithic construction did give rise to the term 'Heliolithic' used to describe the British diffusionists and denoting an ancient people with a Sun-centered religion and construction techniques utilizing massive stones.

In *Gods and Men*, Perry went on to describe the wider academic field within which he intended the book to be read. In this connection, Perry named his own *The Megalithic Culture of Indonesia* (1918), *The Children of the Sun* (1923, 1927), *The Origin of Magic and Religion* (1923), and *The Growth of Civilisation* (1924, 1926). Perry listed these books along with G. Elliot Smith's *The Evolution of the Dragon* (1919), C. Daryll Forde's *Ancient Mariners* (1927), and A. M. Hocart's *Kingship* (1927).[156] Perry believed that when taken together, these works were forming the basis for a solid study of what he called the "archaic civilization".

---

[154] Ibid., 56. Djedkare Isesi is also known as Tancheres by the ancient Greeks. Some suggest that during his reign, the deity Osiris was ascendant rather than Ra.

[155] Ibid., 72-73.

[156] Ibid., 87.

In 1924, W. J. Perry further clarified his diffusionist views and his identification of the archaic civilization. Perry contended that, in terms of social organization, the archaic civilization was categorized as a stage beyond food gathering—in fact, he believed this group had moved on to food producing by settled agriculture.[157] Two years later, Perry's book *The Growth of Civilisation* was revised and, in it, Perry thanked V. Gordon Childe for his participation and assistance with the work. Childe, an eminent archeologist, was not to distance himself from the school of diffusionism until the later 1950s. At roughly the same time, following a relatively productive period, Perry contributed little else to the diffusionist movement due to an extended illness which eventually took his life. Yet, by that time, Perry had already added his incredibly popular and most widely-read work *The Children of the Sun*.

W. J. Perry pointed out in *The Children of the Sun*, that many anthropologists had misapplied Darwin's biological theory to the social realm.[158] Perry said that his opponent's "hypothesis of spontaneous development of culture in all places…fails to take account of the movements of culture that have obviously taken place."[159] Together Perry and Elliot Smith placed human selectivity and behavior at the center of change rather than blind natural forces as the key determinants of cultural developments.[160]

---

[157] W. J. Perry, "Appendix III: The Dual Organization," in W. H. R. Rivers, Social Organization, (London: Kegan Paul, Trench, Trubner, 1924), 207. Thus, Perry helped provide a definition and locus for the precursors to civilization.

[158] W. J. Perry, The Children of the Sun, (New York: E. P. Dutton and Company, 1923), 413-414.

[159] Ibid., 414.

[160] Ibid.

Since evolutionary processes could not be applied to culture, Perry was convinced that only very few geographical areas could have been the sites of original cultural innovations that eventually led to the curious complex of traits called civilization.

It is important to recognize that based upon then known and accepted chronologies, Perry dismissed as areas of early cultural innovation, development, and diffusion: India, Oceania, and North America. Essentially through this process, Perry eliminated all except Egypt and Sumer.[161] Perry clarified this when he wrote, "I do not mean that every element was necessarily invented by the Egyptians: I mean that it took shape in Egypt and was propagated thence."[162] Perry claimed that at the beginning of the Fifth Dynasty in Egypt, the original 'Children of the Sun' emerged and with their expansion and cultural contacts, other areas of the East were exposed to those beliefs.[163] He also considered the unification of Egypt to be a key to the diffusion of these cultural traits.[164] This is presumably because this signal event was an impetus to culture contact, as unification entailed a critical stimulation of creativity and subsequent population movements.

Throughout *The Children of the Sun*, Perry cited the work of contemporary competent specialists such as Arthur Evans, E. M. Siret, and Joseph Dechelette.[165] Based upon their studies, Perry claimed that warfare "began in a highly organized condition of society, and thus is not a fundamental mode of behaviour common

---

[161] Ibid., 428.

[162] Ibid.

[163] Ibid., 165.

[164] Ibid., 429.

[165] Ibid., 499.

to mankind. If the arguments advanced here be [are] correct, it follows that warfare is the outcome of social institutions that can be modified, and thus the problem of its abolition is ultimately soluble."[166] This speaks to the critique of his contemporary society and the reaction to World War I that appears to have been a major motivation for Perry in his studies of the earliest forms of human societies, specifically those he believed to be incapable of large-scale conflict and social violence.

Perry contended that a fundamental element to the emergence of the archaic civilization was rooted in settled agriculture and specifically grain/maize cultivation as rudiments of a more sedentary society, which he thought led to the ability of societies to organize large groups of people and engage in massive social discord.[167] Explaining further, Perry noted, "It is an error, as profound as it is universal, to think that men in the food-gathering stage were given to fighting. All the available facts go to show that the food-gathering stage of history must have been one of perfect peace."[168] Ultimately, Perry said of the archaic civilization, "Maybe that some of the problems that face us at the present day will find their solution in the determination of the reasons that brought to ruins this civilization that was so rich in material culture."[169]

Perry was thus contradicting then current social psychology that explained modern violence and warfare by projecting it into humanity's ancient past and, by implication, asserting that this behavior was innate to humankind, leaving warfare as an

---

[166] Ibid., 4.

[167] Ibid., 102.

[168] Ibid., 154.

[169] Ibid., 163.

inevitability and an intrinsic component of the human future.[170] Perry was joined in these efforts for a short time by W. H. R. Rivers and more extensively by Elliot Smith, both of whom adhered to very similar interpretations. By making such arguments, the trio exposed themselves to notable levels of criticism.

Smith and Egypt

Clearly, G. Elliot Smith's views agreed in many ways with those of Rivers and Perry. He believed the Egyptians were a peaceful, autochthonous Nilotic group.[171] Elliot Smith disagreed with the 'foreign invasion' theories of many contemporary archeologists. For him, this was mainly because G. A. Reisner's findings conclusively ended any such debate and established local origins for Egyptians. Elliot Smith believed that the hypothesis of diffusionism stood on solid scientific ground following the analysis by Reisner which supported his claims of the lack of violent clashes among the earliest Egyptians.[172]

Elliot Smith had long desired to work with Rivers to establish their claims regarding the Egyptian culture diffusion and related this to Perry, Rivers, and his own antipathy to warfare. As early as 1916, Rivers was offered an opportunity to accomplish greater work with more influence as Manchester's Professor of Comparative Religion. However, Rivers was too busy during the war to accept.[173] Later, in 1922, Elliot Smith attempted to get

---

[170] Ibid., 239.

[171] G. E. Smith, <u>The Ancient Egyptians and the Origin of Civilization</u>, (Freeport, New York: Books for Libraries Press, 1923, 1970), 43.

[172] Ibid., 111.

Rivers to take on UCL's Readership in Cultural Anthropology.[174] Elliot Smith had created this position loosely connected with the Department of Anatomy (which Smith chaired at the time).[175] Elliot Smith wanted Rivers and himself to demonstrate that the emergence of civilization was "like the addition of one link after another to a chain, or series of chains, that stretched...from Egypt to India to China and out through the Pacific islands to the higher centers of civilization in the New World."[176]

The British diffusionists were not alone in tracing the possibility of the ancient movements of the Egyptians, which did not always mean direct implantation of ideas, but rather more mitigated contacts wherein the receiving culture adapted the ideas to their preexisting beliefs and made their own modifications. In fact, Osbert Guy Stanhope Crawford (1886-1957), who studied at Oxford, and Robert Eric Mortimer Wheeler (1890-1976), of the University of London, were archeologists involved in similar endeavors. These studies of cultural interchange and modification were useful to the Heliolithic diffusionists, but were ignored by later writers as if those works had never existed. Nevertheless, we shall next examine the diffusionist notions of interchange and societal modification as they were developed by the Heliolithic school of thought.

---

[173] Ian Langham, <u>The Building of British Social Anthropology: W. H. R. Rivers and His Cambridge Disciples in the Development of Kinship Studies, 1898-1931</u>, (Boston, Mass.: D. Reidel, 1981), 352, n. 91.

[174] Ibid., 357, n. 85.

[175] Ibid., 146.

[176] Fred W. Voget, <u>A History of Ethnology</u>, (New York: Holt, Rinehart, and Winston, 1975), 343-344.

CHAPTER FIVE

CULTURE MOVEMENT AND ADAPTATION

Grafton Elliot Smith's utmost early concern was with "understanding human mental evolution".[177] G. E. Smith quickly became the 'world's leading comparative neurologist' and later applied his knowledge gained from these studies to culture diffusion.[178] Smith claimed that T. H. Huxley's writings determined his "chief interests" from mental evolution to the emergence and dispersal of civilization.[179] Indeed, Smith even modeled many of his early studies upon those suggested by Huxley's notes and other works. He believed he had found within Huxley's work the same desire that he held regarding an essential unity of knowledge, particularly the sciences. Elliot Smith went as far as to credit Huxley with shaping anthropology.[180] He even declared a "deep debt" of personal obligation to Huxley stemming from holding a similar position in his time and an overall affinity for very similar research.[181] Some of G. E. Smith's early work prompted G.

---

[177] Raymond A. Dart, "Sir Grafton Elliot Smith and the Evolution of Man," in A. P. Elkin and N. W. G. Macintosh, eds., <u>Grafton Elliot Smith: The Man and His Work</u>, (Portland, Oregon: International Scholarly Book Services, 1974), 26.

[178] Ibid., 28.

[179] Grafton Elliot Smith, <u>Conversion in Science</u>, (Great Britain: Richard Clay and Sons, Limited, Bungay, Suffolk, 1929), 2.

[180] Grafton Elliot Smith, <u>The Place of Thomas Henry Huxley in Anthropology—The Huxley Memorial Lecture for 1935</u>, (London: Royal Anthropological Institute of Great Britain and Ireland, 1935), 3.

B. Howes to turn over Huxley's notes and research for completion because Howes also recognized the expertise of Elliot Smith and the relation between Smith and Huxley's work. According to Smith, Huxley insisted that evolution was a useful explanatory notion only in biological development rather than the realm of economic, political, or social affairs—this was one element that Smith always retained in his own work, as did Perry and Rivers.[182]

G. E. Smith was, additionally, influenced by biological theories regarding the debates surrounding the issue of race. For instance, he accepted that categorical distinctions could be made between racial groups, which was a very common notion in his day. Early in his career, Elliot Smith believed that racial distinctions could be made through the analysis of bone structures and other general anthropometrical methods. However, Elliot Smith was very critical of Aryan racialist claims.[183] Smith further denied the existence of any such race and declared it nothing more than a fiction.[184] This is in contradistinction to some of the claims made by recent histories of anthropology which have a couple of times attempted to paint Elliot Smith as a racist. Yet, as will become clear, that is entirely contrary to the facts.

Elliot Smith's comments on the issue of race were prescient when he called the racist claims prevalent in his day, "…a peculiarly noxious fallacy, which has been recently resuscitated in Germany

---

[181] Ibid.

[182] Ibid., 4.

[183] Smith, "Nordic Race Claims," Appendix B, in W. R. Dawson, ed., Sir Grafton Elliot Smith: A Biographical Record by His Colleagues, (London: Cape, 1938), 260. Dawson included this reprint version from 1934 and 1938.

[184] Ibid., 261.

for a new career of evil."[185] Furthermore, Smith said, "We have a sufficient mass of exact evidence today to be sure that the claims made for the Nordic strain are devoid of any adequate justification."[186] Yet, Elliot Smith still maintained for a time that some global racial distinctions could be made in order to study the movements of past populations. It is important to note this because many modern detractors, often isolationists, attempt to label all diffusionism as a guise of racism. G. E. Smith, however, abjured racism and preferred to concentrate on the astounding accomplishments of the early Egyptians.

Apparently, Elliot Smith's attention was first drawn toward Egypt by the suggestion of W. H. R. Rivers.[187] While researching in Egypt, Elliot Smith worked with F. Wood Jones and D. E. Derry. Together they compiled anthropometrical data on thousands of predynastic Egyptians—resulting from G. A. Reisner's excavations.[188] This experience allowed Elliot Smith to begin to think in physical comparativist terms, from which he made cultural assumptions. Once he returned to England, Smith was to perform further anatomical and anthropological research and began publication with his eye toward more closely tying together these disparate academic endeavors.

In England, Elliot Smith quickly befriended Professor G. B. Howes (Huxley's successor in Zoology at the Royal College of

---

[185] Smith, "The Aryan Question," Appendix B, in W. R. Dawson, ed., <u>Sir Grafton Elliot Smith</u>, 263. Dawson included this reprint version from 1935 and 1938.

[186] Ibid., 268.

[187] W. H. R. Rivers, <u>Psychology and Politics</u>, (London: Kegan Paul, Trench, Trubner and Company, Inc., 1923), 126.

[188] Dart, "Sir Grafton Elliot Smith," in Elkin and Macintosh, eds., <u>Grafton Elliot Smith</u>, 30.

Science, London later to be the Imperial College of Science), who provided Smith with full access to T. H. Huxley's scientific papers.[189] Between 1894 and 1919, G. E. Smith published numerous original papers on neurological anatomy and physiology. Smith's final contributions, in this sense, were in the seventh edition of Daniel John Cunningham's *Textbook of Anatomy* (1937).[190] It was prior to this, however, that G. E. Smith began formulating a theory of culture diffusion.

In January 1923, Grafton Elliot Smith penned the preface for a revised edition of the 1915 work *The Ancient Egyptians and the Origin of Civilization*. This book was intended to coincide with the original publication of W. J. Perry's *The Children of the Sun* (1923). In *The Ancient Egyptians*, G. E. Smith intended, "...to open up a new view—or rather to revive and extend an old and neglected method of interpretation—of the history of civilization...."[191] Smith

---

[189] P. O. Bishop, "Grafton Elliot Smith's Contribution to Visual Neurology and the Influence of Thomas Henry Huxley," in Elkin and Macintosh, eds., Grafton Elliot Smith, 53.

[190] Ibid., 54. Elliot Smith was very indecisive as to what to call this group.

[191] Grafton Elliot Smith, The Ancient Egyptians and the Origin of Civilization, (Freeport, New York: Books for Libraries Press, [1923], 1970), v. Elliot Smith, for his Ships as Evidence of the Migrations of Early Culture (1917), relied on Holmes' "Ancient and Modern Ships" (1900). He also cited a series of works by Keble Chatterton (1878-1944) such as: Sailing the Seas: A Survey of Seafaring through the Ages (1931), On the High Seas (1929), Daring Deeds of Sea Rovers: An Account of the Stirring Adventures of Sea Routers from the Times of the Phoenicians, Egyptians, and Vikings, Through the Elizabethan and All Other Eras of Maritime Roving Down to the Present Day (1929), Across the Seven Seas (1927), The Ship under Sail: The Splendour of the Sailing Ship through the Ages (1926), and Sailing Ships: The Story of Their Development from the Earliest Times to the Present Day (1909). To reiterate, it can readily be seen that Elliot Smith was relying on contemporary source material for his claims.

was referring to the diffusionist perspective to which he believed certain physical traits could be related and the movements of peoples and ideas traced.

Elliot Smith believed that his analysis of physical traits pointed to a Nilotic origin for Egyptian civilization.[192] The physical forms that Smith believed he had discerned were identified as "Giza" traits. This was a position Elliot Smith later modified to account for other physical possibilities as he began to move beyond the 'essentialist' viewpoint, and to a limited extent typological, conception of humanity, which he felt was suggested in the works of Huxley. Many of these conclusions were supported in the works of W. J. Perry and Rivers.

According to Elliot Smith, by 1918 his colleague W. H. R. Rivers had come to accept a Heliolithic schema of culture movements centered in Egypt.[193] Elliot Smith also noted that he believed that coming from the sciences, craniological and other physical feature studies were as definitive as any evidence from other areas of investigation and that this fell precisely within his own field of expertise and in support of diffusion from Egypt to surrounding areas.[194] More than this, Elliot Smith took numerous opportunities to mention his personal disagreement with German 'Aryan' race theories that were becoming prevalent at the time.[195] Smith was more interested in establishing the parameters of Egyptian culture contacts and population movement as opposed to imaginative claims of superiority and the like.

---

[192] Smith, Conversion in Science, 36.

[193] Smith, The Ancient Egyptians and the Origin of Civilization, vii.

[194] Ibid., viii.

[195] Smith, The Place of Thomas Henry Huxley in Anthropology, 4-5.

Even in *The Ancient Egyptians and the Origin of Civilization*, G. E. Smith was careful to point out that anthropologists must allow for the possibility of indirect cultural influence due to the rapid treks of surrounding societies.[196] Contrary to common mischaracterizations by some of his contemporaries and later critics, Elliot Smith did not assert Egyptians traveled to, for example, the Americas and directly implanted cultural innovations. Additionally, Rivers in various lectures tried to stress just this point but it apparently has still not been noted by most anthropologists or those writing the history of the discipline. Rivers went further and often insisted that the travelers spurring culture change need not have been Egyptians in each instance.[197] Rather, over time and distance, other societies passed on distinctive culture traits—all of which had been modified by the interacting cultures. Indeed, for Elliot Smith only the "germs of the civilization" emerged in Egypt and then extended to other regions.[198]

Elliot Smith explicitly stated his position when he wrote, "…it must not be assumed that the Egyptians themselves were directly responsible for spreading their great inventions abroad throughout the world."[199] In clarification, he added that Egyptians likely only traversed as far as Sumer and that in-between there emerged a number of unique, secondary diffusion centers.[200] This explanation entailed neither racial affinities nor pockets of colonizing or conquering Egyptians. Above all, Elliot Smith

---

[196] Smith, Ancient Egyptians, viii-ix.

[197] Rivers, Psychology and Politics, 130-131.

[198] Smith, Ancient Egyptians, ix.

[199] Ibid., xii.

[200] Ibid.

described the Egyptian's mode of behavior and artifacts in terms of the fulfillment of some function perhaps even opening the path (or at least acknowledging) that anthropology would later take with the dominance of structural-functionalism.[201] It is in this limited sense that his theories anticipated those of diffusion's successors, which may come as a surprise to some who have not studied the entirety of G.E. Smith's writings on the subject. It was perhaps Smith's interest in the function of artifacts and behavior that in time led him to make alterations to his diffusion theory because his diffusionist concepts were not identical from the first book to the last.

Elliot Smith's theory, as it developed in later years, was to move away from the more or less single-mindedly "Egyptocentric," conceptualization as he began to proclaim a more generalized process of movements and adaptations from southwest Asia and northern Africa. There was, in fact, no racially specific group for this argument as it was elaborated and Smith repeatedly insisted that he did not mean the Egyptian group directly transplanted their cultural traits among other societies, for example, in the Americas. According to the British diffusionists, any trait adopted was also adapted and modified by the receiving society in order to fit within the new social context and was propagated after that.[202]

Darwin's Enemies

Elliot Smith was fervently committed to biological evolutionism, which is key because critics claim that diffusionists of almost all stripes were part of a more general reaction against Darwinian evolution. This is another form of modernist

---

[201] Elkin, "Elliot Smith and the Diffusion of Culture," in Elkin and Macintosh, eds., <u>Grafton Elliot Smith</u>, 141.

[202] Ibid., 142.

argumentation which attempts to inure anthropologists against the consideration of wide-ranging cultural diffusion. Because of this commitment and Adolph Bastian's association with the anti-evolutionist views of Rudolph Virchow (1821-1902), Bastian's arguments met with derision repeatedly in G. E. Smith's work. Moreover, Elliot Smith noted that Fritz Graebner and Wilhelm Schmidt's theological motives caused them to reject anything associated with evolutionism and this prejudiced the British diffusionists against the German school diffusion.[203] Thus, although the *kulturkreis* school was diffusionist in outlook, their relationship to an anti-evolutionist approach in terms of both the biological and the social made them unacceptable in the eyes of the British diffusionists.

In *The Diffusion of Culture*, G. E. Smith had gathered together quite a following among fellow academics and attempted to establish a more suitable form of diffusion.[204] This 1933 book was partially compiled and prepared with help from W. J. Perry, C. D. Forde, and H. J. Massingham. In this particular work, W. H. R. Rivers was referred to as an ethnologist which one can take as a label of praise for his overall academic contributions beyond the field of psychology.[205] There were, however, more pertinent problems confronting Elliot Smith within the domain of anthropological theory and in his popular book *Elephants and Ethnologists*, he analyzed twenty-eight major source books (dating from 1813 to 1921) that discussed the various possibilities for cultural diffusion.[206] Herein G. E. Smith mentioned the arguments put

---

[203] Grafton Elliot Smith, The Diffusion of Culture, (London: Watts and Company, 1933), 237-238.

[204] Ibid., v.

[205] Ibid., 36.

forth against Charles Darwin's evolutionary theory, perhaps attempting to class his diffusionist theory with biological evolutionism.[207] That is in the sense that Smith perceived great opposition to both ideas from many in both the public and within academia or at least he rhetorically positioned the argument in that fashion. He was adamantly convinced of the correctness of both biological evolutionism and cultural diffusionism as a foundation for future scientific studies. Elliot Smith also went so far as to cast the diffusion controversy in terms of the opposition faced by Galileo and subtly hinted that he would likely be proven correct over time.[208] However, Elliot Smith was also disturbed with the interminable problems with dating discrepancies and the relative dating scheme available at the time, which caused him to always leave open the possibility that he and his fellow diffusionists were incorrect on a number of points. He did not, however, feel that an alteration in the dating schema would utterly undermine the general concept of vast cultural diffusion.

In addition to admitting the possibility that he was incorrect on some specifics and relating his work to that of Darwin, Elliot Smith also wished to resurrect the philosophy of history found in the works of Anne-Robert-Jacques Turgot (1727-1781).[209] Smith contended there was a connection between his philosophy of science and philosophy of history, both of which he attempted to delineate in his diffusion works. G. E. Smith was particularly fond of Turgot's 1750 discourse *Progres Successifs de l'Esprit Humain*, which

---

[206] Grafton Elliot Smith, Elephants and Ethnologists, (New York: E. P. Dutton and Company, 1924), 12-19.

[207] Ibid., 2.

[208] Ibid., 109.

[209] Smith, Conversion in Science, 4-30.

proffered a cyclical notion of the rise and demise of civilization.[210] The oscillatory interchange of "progress" and "barbarism" was prominent throughout most of Elliot Smith's later works. In his *magnum opus*, *Human History*, G. E. Smith stated, "It is the aim of this book once more to revive Turgot's fruitful philosophy."[211] Smith coupled this with his objections to certain historians who he believed had a negative impact on the views of humanity's collective past which, to him, seemed to laud aggression, conflict, and violence.

Elliot Smith was disturbed by the wide popularity of English historian Henry Thomas Buckle's *History of Civilization in England* (1857-1861).[212] In this book, H. T. Buckle (1821-1862) had supported cultural isolationism, Cartesianism, positivism, and by implication, psychic unity or the independent development of the world's various cultures. Nothing could have been more anathema to Elliot Smith than this combination of wrong-headed beliefs, because he believed that this constellation of ideas was directly related to the opposition of a diffusionist perspective. Smith took exception to Buckle's claims and thus countered them in his own massive tome, *Human History*. Unlike Buckle, Elliot Smith rejected both determinist and positivist notions of universal laws that could be discerned from history and then be applied to the development of 'human nature'. Elliot Smith's work also countered other larger trends in Britain that tended to obscure humanistic visions of Africa, which he coupled with his rejection of Cartesianism, positivism, and isolationism. Yet Smith was still not finished with

---

[210] Smith, Human History, 38.

[211] Ibid., 39.

[212] Elkin, "Elliot Smith and the Diffusion of Culture," in Elkin and Macintosh, eds., Grafton Elliot Smith, 152.

correcting the damage he felt had been done by Buckle and others who interpreted history in a similar way.

Epistemologically, Elliot Smith drew on the works of Frederick John Teggart (1870-1946) for much of his opposition to Buckle's Cartesianism. F. J. Teggart's 1925 publication of *Theory of History* and later, "The Humanistic Study of Change in Time" (1926), led Elliot Smith to new philosophical considerations of history and science.[213] This further led Smith to oppose the intellectual approaches of Aristotle, Ptolemy, Galen, and, especially, Descartes.[214] In contrast to their views, G. E. Smith offered Copernicus, Galileo, Newton, and Darwin as providing sound philosophies of science and history for humanity.[215]

G. E. Smith also attempted to counter arguments of independent cultural evolution, which assumed that so-called "progressing" cultures would develop along the same lines and experience similar stages or phases while moving from a 'primitive' state upwards to civilization. Elliot Smith was angered by the fact that this outline implied the psychic unity of humankind. Smith also identified the problem of determinist tendencies in the philosophy of history proffered by Jean Bodin (1530-1596) in his *Method for the Easy Comprehension of History* (1566). Bodin set about a path that Smith found to be increasingly confusing for all who attempted to apply Bodin's deterministic methodology. This method included a combination of climatic determinism and progressionism with a defense of authoritarian or autocratic notions, similar to those espoused by Comte, which G. E. Smith believed was related to the views of social evolutionists and social

---

[213] Ibid.

[214] Smith, Conversion in Science, 20.

[215] Ibid., 2.

Darwinists.²¹⁶ In many of these arguments, Smith was joined by Perry. ²¹⁷ W. J. Perry, who for the most part refrained from criticizing functionalism, much like Elliot Smith opposed climatic/environmental determinism.²¹⁸ Perry repudiated environmental determinist theories and attempted to relate this opposition with broader issues in anthropology leaning more towards a concept of human agency rather than a more strictly determinist perspective.²¹⁹

Ethnicity

Notable for its influence on G. E. Smith's theory of culture movement and adaptation, was Giuseppe Sergi's (1841-1936) *La Stirpe Mediterranea* (1895), which was released in England in 1901 under the title *The Mediterranean Race: A Study of the Origin of European Peoples.*²²⁰ More importantly, Sergi's book celebrated multi-ethnic heritages, rather than misleading concepts of "purity" as advocated by racialists and herediterians. Sergi was vehemently opposed to racial supremacists, Nordicists, and master race theorists. Importantly, for diffusionism, Sergi also postulated the existence of a 'Mediterranean race with its centre in North Africa,

---

²¹⁶ Smith, Conversion in Science, 35-36.

²¹⁷ Elkin, "Elliot Smith and the Diffusion of Culture", in Elkin and Macintosh, eds., Grafton Elliot Smith, 145.

²¹⁸ W. J. Perry, The Children of the Sun, (New York: E. P. Dutton and Company, 1923), 408-409; Elkin, "Elliot Smith and the Diffusion of Culture," in Elkin and Macintosh, eds., Grafton Elliot Smith, 156, n. 14.

²¹⁹ Perry, The Children of the Sun, 92-93.

²²⁰ Daniel, 150 Years of Archaeology, (Cambridge, Mass.: Harvard University Press, 1975), 180.

which spread all over the Mediterranean region'. A very similar notion was supported by Arthur Evans (1851-1941) in his *Eastern Question in Anthropology* (1895).[221] Not incidentally, the year 1895 also witnessed John Myres' publication of *Prehistoric Man in the Eastern Mediterranean* with a very similar conceptual outline.[222] Each of these works found their way into Elliot Smith and Perry's research programs, which balanced their interpretations of the conceptualization of race and ethnicity. Sergi's work broadened Smith's perspective of the possible involvement of a number of culture groups in the process of diffusion.

As his theories developed further, Elliot Smith began to consider and discuss the possibility of Indo-Chinese impacts on the Americas. He postulated multiple Asiatic and/or Indian diffusionary waves that took place in the Pre-Columbian context.[223] Nevertheless, Smith found more importance in the localized effects of Egypt, Babylonia, and India upon one another rather than transoceanic impacts.[224] Smith was careful to note that none of these influences occurred without adaptation and assimilation.[225] In this connection, he pointed out that in the early 1920s, "The leading archaeologists admit the debt of Crete to Egypt, and many of them realize that Syria also derived its cultural capital from Egypt."[226] In 1929, Elliot Smith contended that the Americas, Asia, and Oceania

---

[221] Ibid.

[222] Ibid., 180-181.

[223] Ibid., 99.

[224] Ibid., 122-123.

[225] Ibid., 124.

[226] Smith, <u>Conversion in Science</u>, 36.

received only indirect cultural influences from Egypt.²²⁷ This kind of caution may even be found in some of Smith's earlier writings despite some of the attacks from later histories of anthropology which primarily refer to works written around 1910-1912.²²⁸

Being more careful than his critics suggest, G. E. Smith noted that "maritime trafficking" amongst two groups does not mean that any significant culture diffusion took place.²²⁹ In *The Influence of Ancient Egyptian Civilization in the East and in America*, Elliot Smith claimed that Egyptians affected Eastern Mediterranean islands and coasts. Subsequently, he said, close to the end of the 'New Empire' or later, Phoenicians spread elements of this culture abroad. Slowly, these groups progressed to 'India, Further Asia, the Malay Archipelago, Oceania, and America'. Therefore, the connection to the Americas was only indirect and spread out over time.²³⁰ While attempting to avoid being dogmatic, promoted numerous centers of secondary diffusion: the Indus, Sumer, Asia Minor, and Crete.²³¹

On several occasions, Elliot Smith emphasized that his claims were not meant to be taken as absolutes; rather these claims were only offered as tentative possibilities subject to greater study and further modification yet not complete refutation. Smith asserted that the Heliolithic complex was composed of culture

---

²²⁷ Ibid., 36.

²²⁸ Grafton Elliot Smith, Elephants and Ethnologists, (London: Kegan Paul, Trench, Trubner and Company, Limited, 1924), 113-125.

²²⁹ Ibid., 6-7.

²³⁰ Grafton Elliot Smith, The Influence of Ancient Egyptian Civilization in the East and in America, (Manchester: The University Press, 1916), 3.

²³¹ Grafton Elliot Smith, Culture: The Diffusion Controversy, (London: Kegan Paul, Trench, Trubner, and Company Limited, 1928), 14-17.

element accretions from Phoenicia, East Africa (specifically the Sudan region), Arabia, Babylonia, and later Indian influences.[232] In diffusionary population movements, Elliot Smith believed there were connections between these geographical areas due to the appearance and confluence of serpent, sky, and sun symbolism.[233] Furthermore, Smith contended that ship construction advancements between the broad expanse of 4000 BCE to 2800 BCE contributed to such culture movements.

Even as early as his publication of the rarely referenced *Primitive Men* (1916-1917), G. E. Smith called for a closer blend of history and prehistory.[234] This book was prescient, for it contained many of the later views that Smith and Perry were to further clarify in their diffusion writings. In this work, Elliot Smith demonstrated that he was a thorough believer in genetic and populational crossings in a strictly Darwinian sense.[235] Smith's paleoanthropological works functioned in support of the theory of diffusion, which he saw as stretching deep into the human past.[236] The British diffusionist's contemporary detractors and recent modernist histories of anthropology have, however, ignored such aspects. In relation to their detractors, it is now necessary to analyze the emergence of anthropology's structural-functionalist paradigm and the transition from social evolutionism and diffusion.

---

[232] Ibid., 4.

[233] Ibid., 5.

[234] Grafton Elliot Smith, <u>Primitive Men</u>, (London: Oxford University Press, 1916-1917), 1-3.

[235] Ibid.

[236] Ibid., 11.

CHAPTER SIX

FROM EVOLUTIONISM TO STRUCTURAL-FUNCTIONALISM

Alfred Cort Haddon (1855-1940), along with W. H. R. Rivers, was part of the first generation of post-Darwinian zoologists and anthropologists—both were thoroughgoing biological evolutionists.[237] Haddon flirted with diffusionism, but never in the sense of Elliot Smith or Perry. Rivers, on the other hand, was keenly interested in establishing a biological basis for psychological problems exhibited in human society. This attempt is exemplified in his *Instinct and the Unconscious* (1920).[238] Rivers also helped move anthropologists beyond simplistic conceptions of "primitive thought" that had often been conceived of as "pre-logical" by ethnocentric theorists.[239] Ironically, Rivers' role as an educator put him into contact with some whom later as structural-functionalists opposed diffusion.

In 1893, Rivers was selected to instruct the physiology of sense perception at Cambridge and, four years later, he was elected to a Lectureship in Physiological and Experimental Psychology.[240] Rivers was also involved in the establishment of England's first

---

[237] James Urry, Before Social Anthropology: Essays on the History of British Anthropology, (Reading: Harwood Academic Publishers, 1993), 63.

[238] W. H. R. Rivers, Instinct and the Unconscious: A Contribution to a Biological Theory of the Psycho-Neuroses, (Cambridge: Cambridge University Press, 1922), 1-21 passim.

[239] George Stocking, Jr., After Tylor: British Social Anthropology, 1888-1951, (Madison, Wisconsin: University of Wisconsin Press, 1995), 236.

[240] Urry, Before Social Anthropology , 76.

psychological laboratories at Cambridge in 1897 and London in 1898.[241] Many students were drawn to Rivers because of his many academic accomplishments and his compelling personality and charisma.

During this period (1893-1898), Rivers advanced psychological studies of sense perception geared towards a more cross-cultural approach.[242] G. E. Smith and Rivers made contact and began their friendship as early as an 1896 meeting at Cambridge.[243] Rivers was Praelector of Natural Science Studies by 1919.[244] Earlier, he received a Gold Medal of the Royal Society in 1915, and also became the first president of the British Psychoanalytical Society in 1919, president of the Folk-Lore Society (1921-1922), and president of the Royal Anthropological Institute in 1922.[245] According to historian of anthropology James Urry, "[It] was Rivers with his advocacy of history and diffusion who made the final break with nineteenth century evolutionism (Rivers, 1911)."[246]

---

[241] Graham D. Richards, "William Halse Rivers (1864-1922)," *The Psychologist* 14, no. 9, (September 2001): 464.

[242] Ibid.

[243] Henrika Kuklick, The Savage Within: The Social History of British Anthropology, 1885-1945, (New York: Cambridge University Press, 1992), 128; Ian Langham, The Building of British Social Anthropology: W. H. R. Rivers and His Cambridge Disciples in the Development of Kinship Studies, 1898-1931, (Boston, Mass.: D. Reidel, 1981), 135; Stocking, After Tylor, 210.

[244] Langham, The Building of British Social Anthropology, 53.

[245] George Stocking, Jr., Functionalism Historicized: Essays on British Social Anthropology, (Madison, Wisconsin: University of Wisconsin Press, 1984), 58-74.

[246] Urry, Before Social Anthropology, 79. By which Urry meant social evolutionism.

Together Elliot Smith and Rivers, "reasoned, the origin of a new civilization was an unpredictable, chance variation, just as the origin of a new species was."[247] According to Henrika Kuklick, professor of the history of human sciences and the sociology of science, "Their scheme incorporated a general theoretical framework that appealed to an audience far larger than avowed diffusionists—an audience that included other members of the anthropological community as well as persons outside it."[248] And, as a noteworthy contrast to many of the unilinear social evolutions of the day, Smith and Rivers emphasized the role of indeterminacy in culture change and this notion has been useful to later anthropologists.[249]

In terms of later anthropological developments, it is important to note that Rivers "was the man who, more than any other, diverted the attention of British anthropologists from the evolution of religious thought to the synchronic functioning of single societies."[250] In addition, Adam Kuper has referred to Rivers as the "greatest figure of the pre-functionalist" era.[251] Thus, it is ironic that Rivers is sometimes (and probably correctly) listed among the precursors for the theory of structural-functionalism that was to seize the field of anthropology from the diffusionists.

---

[247] Kuklick, The Savage Within, 126.

[248] Ibid., 124.

[249] Bruce Trigger, A History of Archaeological Thought, (New York: Cambridge University Press, 1989), 250.

[250] Langham, The Building of British Social Anthropology, 50.

[251] Adam Kuper, Anthropologists and Anthropology: The Modern British School, 1922-1972, (New York: Routledge, 1996), 9.

It may even be argued that some of Rivers' works lead directly to the emergence of the successor to evolutionism, though that may be overstating the case a bit, being the structural-functionalism as delineated in the works of Bronislaw Malinowski and A. R. Radcliffe-Brown. By many accounts, A. R. Radcliffe-Brown was inspired to anthropology by A. C. Haddon and W. H. R. Rivers.[252] Radcliffe-Brown also owed intellectual allegiance to Comte and Spencer on "their distinction between social statics and social dynamics".[253] In this framework, the conceptualization of "static" related to psychological aspects whereas the term "dynamic" related to historical subjects.[254] Radcliffe-Brown made elaborate analogies between social organization and anatomical/physiological arrangement of human organisms.[255] In this, Radcliffe-Brown believed that the focus should be on 'social statics' or a psychological basis for the multiply components of human society. 'Utility' and 'immediate social function' were among his preeminent concerns.[256] These concerns, it should be noted, also interested those that funded anthropological research because demonstrable utilitarian results could be attained; this necessity was followed by both Radcliffe-Brown and Malinowski in their works although their personal interests were not exactly reflected by the institutions that controlled the distribution of research and lectureship funds.[257]

---

[252] Urry, <u>Before Social Anthropology</u>, 121.

[253] Ibid., 122.

[254] Ibid.

[255] Ibid., 123.

[256] Ibid.

[257] Ibid., 123-126.

From 1906 to 1908, Radcliffe-Brown performed fieldwork in the Andaman Islands and utilized some aspects of Rivers' genealogical method in his own analysis. With this, he also combined the sociological influence of Emile Durkheim. Radcliffe-Brown still focused on kinship studies in his 1910 to 1912 studies of the Kariera, an Australian aborigine people. In an adventitious connection, G. E. Smith and the prominent Bohemian anthropologist working in the United States, Ales Hrdlicka (1869-1943), had an ongoing correspondence, wherein Hrdlicka advocated the appointment of a physical anthropologist to a key post in Sydney rather than Elliot Smith's suggestion of a social anthropologist.[258] The ironic selection of the social anthropologist Radcliffe-Brown may have been one of the earliest fractures between Elliot Smith and Hrdlicka, one that also did not help in the propagation of diffusionist theory.[259] Grafton Elliot Smith along with A. C. Haddon selected A. R. Radcliffe-Brown over "the historical diffusionist A. M. Hocart" for a professorship at the University of Sydney.[260] There are a number of similarities between the work of Radcliffe-Brown and his contemporary Bronislaw Malinowski.

Emerging at nearly the same time, Malinowski's work was 'antihistorical', and influenced by Freudian psychoanalysis,

---

[258] N. W. G. Macintosh, "An Appreciation," in A. P. Elkin and N. W. G. Macintosh, eds., Grafton Elliot Smith: The Man and His Work, (Portland, Oregon: International Scholarly Book Services, 1974), 18. It is beyond the scope of the current work to discuss other issues involving Hrdlicka, but in the next volume of this series those issues will be prominent and discussed at length.

[259] Ironic because though G. E. Smith desired the appointment, it went to an opponent of diffusion.

[260] George W. Stocking, Jr., ed., Objects and Others: Essays on Museums and Material Culture, (Madison, Wisconsin: The University of Wisconsin Press, 1985), 120.

Frazerian anthropology, Durkheim, Edward Westermarck, Ernst Mach, and Tylorian evolutionism.[261] All were figures that the diffusionists criticized. Malinowski spent fifteen years at the London School of Economics and reigned "as the only master ethnographer", according to Adam Kuper.[262] Yet, the American Clyde Kluckholn, at one time, said Malinowski was credulous and pretentious, and suggested that Malinowski's works were nowhere near as objective and scientific as he and his followers frequently proclaimed.[263] Nevertheless, a number of ethnologists still tended to prefer diffusionism and sociologists were inclined toward social evolutionary schema, which show that there was great variation in Malinowski's day regarding what was considered the objective scientific standard.[264]

It has been demonstrated by preeminent historian of anthropology George W. Stocking, Jr. and others, that Radcliffe-Brown derived much from Rivers.[265] Edward Evans-Pritchard in his own work on the history of anthropology stated that Rivers influenced both Malinowski and Radcliffe-Brown to an extent.[266] In

---

[261] George Stocking, Jr., <u>Victorian Anthropology</u>, (New York: The Free Press, 1991), 321. 'Frazerian' anthropology refers to the work of James George Frazer (1854-1951) famously known for his popular <u>The Golden Bough</u> (1890), which posited a three stage cultural sequence similar to the social evolutionist paradigm.

[262] Kuper, <u>Anthropologists and Anthropology</u>, 13.

[263] Ibid., 37. Indeed this has been demonstrated through later analysis of Malinowski's writings following the publication of his field notes and diaries. This is discussed in the works of George Stocking, Jr. and Bruce Trigger.

[264] Ibid., 15.

[265] Stocking, <u>Functionalism Historicized</u>, 106.

the 1930s, Radcliffe-Brown taught at the Rockefeller established University of Chicago.[267] Radcliffe-Brown was more anti-evolutionary, influenced also by Durkheim, static-synchronic problemitization, the study of social structure, and Spencerian evolutionism.[268] Recently, James Urry lamented that the structural-functionalists had, "rejected the old, broader vision of anthropology" and became a "blinkered generation".[269] Similarly, Anne-Marie de Waal Malefijt's *The Images of Man* reported, "In England, however, ahistorical functionalism for a while overshadowed all other considerations."[270] Finally, Paul Erickson and Liam Murphy have said of Malinowski and Radcliffe-Brown, "By force of personality and intellect, these two figures set British anthropology on a theoretical course far different from the course it had followed in the nineteenth century."[271] These statements point up the rather extraordinary break with previous anthropological schools of thought which tended to be more historical in nature.

Diffusion's Adherents

---

[266] Edward Evans-Pritchard, A History of Anthropological Thought, (New York: Basic Books, 1981), 192-200.

[267] Urry, Before Social Anthropology, 130.

[268] Stocking, Victorian Anthropology, 322.

[269] Ibid., 133-134.

[270] Anne-Marie de Waal Malefijt, The Images of Man, (New York: Alfred A. Knopf, 1974), 180.

[271] Paul Erickson and Liam Murphy, eds., A History of Anthropological Theory, (Orchard Park, New York: Broadview Press, 1998), 99.

Diffusionism retained a number of supporters despite the changes that were taking place within anthropology. For instance, C. K. Meek's work reflected a number of diffusionist themes, particularly his *The Northern Tribes of Nigeria* (1931). Kegan Paul published Meek's book, like many of those of the Heliolithic approach, perhaps due to the popular appeal of diffusionist themes. Moreover, similar diffusionistic arguments appeared in the roughly contemporary work of R. S. Rattray, specifically his 1932 book *The Tribes of the Ashanti Hinterland*.[272] Earlier, in 1922 at Cambridge, one of Rivers' students, William Armstrong (a moderate diffusionist), was chosen for the position of social anthropologist, a selection that allowed diffusionism a slightly longer life span within British anthropology—yet a number of critics were beginning to attain positions at several universities.[273]

Only by the exaggeration of Elliot Smith and Perry's views by their rival schools of thought could the British diffusionists be easily dismissed. Over time, an outline for a pattern of these attacks has emerged from the both diffusionists' contemporary opponents and more recently from some histories of anthropology such as those by Glyn Daniel and Adam Kuper. The following is an example of the distortion of the Heliolithic argument (in other words this is a straw man that critics manufacture): Elliot Smith believed that civilization emerged only once and in Egypt, then through migration and colonization, the Children of the Sun implanted Sun-centered beliefs and megalithic building elements in societies all over the globe.[274] However, in reality, nothing could be further from their views according to their own writings as the

---

[272] Stocking, After Tylor, 388-389.

[273] Ibid., 293.

[274] Marvin Harris, The Rise of Anthropological Theory: A History of Theories of Culture, (New York: Crowell, 1968), 380-390 passim.

theory ultimately developed over time. Their theory has suffered from an unfortunate number of distortions and mischaracterizations because of a refusal to analyze all of the primary source material, rather than a small selection of secondary (and decidedly anti-diffusionist) sources. In fact, the majority of history works on anthropology only cite an exceedingly minimal number of G. E. Smith's or W.J. Perry's scholarly works. Nonetheless, diffusionism has never been totally lacking of other important advocates.

One such defender of a diffusionist position was the archeologist V. Gordon Childe, who successfully faced a number of counter-arguments for decades. V. G. Childe rebutted some of the diffusionist critic's accusations that the position in some way related to racism. During his academic career, Childe pointed to the relationship between isolationism and Hitlerian nationalism and believed that a model of culture diffusion could mitigate against such problems by supplying a more cosmopolitan worldview and best represent the available facts.[275] Childe never completely dismissed the culture historicist or megalithic diffusionary approach; however he did distance himself from such views in his final edition of The Dawn of European Civilisation.[276] Nevertheless, he had expanded the legacy of the approach began by Rivers and his diffusionist colleagues but with his own unique interpretation and representations. Childe's investigations and conclusions fit within the broad outline of the field, as ethnology/anthropology developed roughly from the 1800s to the 1940s in the following order: social evolutionism (both unilinear and multilinear), historical particularism/diffusionism, and structural-functionalism. However, contrary to social evolutionism and diffusionism, British functionalism was primarily ahistorical to a fault because it failed to

---

[275] Trigger, <u>A History of Archaeological Thought</u>, 255.

[276] Ibid., 244.

offer any resolution to the omnipresent question of origins that always comes with the study of anthropology and the human historical past in general.[277] Stated differently, it fails to account for the question of "How did we get here from there?" Though both of the schools of thought with which structural-functionalist anthropology contended did attempt to offer an answer to this question, the structural-functionalists attempted to avoid the matter altogether and shifted the focus of many academicians to a radically different set of questions.

Diffusionist Inundation

Regardless of the development of opposition, a flood of diffusionist works continues to be produced. For example, Charles Elliot Fox made a foray into the diffusion controversy with his book entitled *Threshold of the Pacific* (1924). In a work clearly reminiscent of Rivers' *The History of Melanesian Society*, C. E. Fox frequently cited Dr. Codrington. G. E. Smith stated in the preface to Fox's book that W. H. R. Rivers had become increasingly accepting of Egypt's role in the history of civilization—particularly in 1918, which has important implications for those who study Rivers and write the history of the discipline of anthropology.[278] Apparently, Rivers had found C. E. Fox's 1918 work on San Cristoval as abundantly convincing and in total confirmation of theories he had been privately developing for some years.[279] According to this

---

[277] Kuklick, The Savage Within, 180.

[278] G. E. Smith, "Preface," in C. E. Fox, Threshold of the Pacific: An Account of the Social Organization, Magic, and Religion of the People of San Cristoval in the Solomon Islands, (London: Kegan Paul, Trench, Trubner and Company, Limited and Stephen Austin and Sons, Limited, 1924), v.

[279] Ibid., vi.

account, Rivers, shortly before his death, found Fox's manuscript to the eventual 1924 edition of that work to be amongst the most significant social anthropological field studies yet made.[280]

For significant portions of this nearly four hundred page text, C. E. Fox collaborated with F. H. Drew, a noted authority on the subject.[281] This book formed a part of the "Historical Ethnology" section of the 'History of Civilization' series edited by C. K. Ogden of Magdalene College, Cambridge and published in London by Kegan Paul. Together these individuals formed a part of a larger network that supported a general notion of diffusion, but did not overtly advocate the position as it was generally subtle in presentation. Furthermore, this series was a very ambitious project that intended to present a 'comprehensive synthesis' of the social sciences from ancient times to the present. The 'History of Civilization' series went on to include numerous diffusionary works with Elliot Smith, Rivers, Fox, Childe, Louis Joseph Delaporte on Mesopotamia (Babylonia and Assyria), Gustave Glotz on the ancient Aegean, Donald A. MacKenzie's *The Migration of Symbols*, Alexandre Moret on Egypt and the Nile, and Orientalist Clement Huart, all contributing their own vision—most of which fit within some form of diffusionist interpretive framework.

Clearly demonstrating his position in regard to culture diffusion, C. E. Fox wrote that he had found that the peoples he researched were linked by customs and beliefs much in the way the British diffusionists had argued. Fox even went as far as to identify these Pacific peoples by employing terms similar to those of Perry, pointedly referring to them as the "archaic civilization of Indonesia and elsewhere."[282] Fox accepted the view that these were the

---

[280] Ibid.

[281] Ibid., ix.

seafaring people of the archaic civilization and that their civilization was mainly Egyptian with accretions from other areas.[283] This did not, however, mean that these seafarers were genetically Egyptian but that they had, at some distant point in the past, been influenced by the lifeways developed in ancient Egypt.

Finally, on a related note, it must be pointed out that Rivers' academic lineage was also important in the broader context of diffusionist anthropology. According to Stocking, Cambridge assigned Rivers' student William Armstrong (also a diffusionist) as professor in 1922 over Bronislaw Malinowski.[284] As a moderate diffusionist and adherent to the views of Rivers, Armstrong may be counted loosely among the Heliolithic school's lineage along with T. T. Barnard, John Layard, and Bernard Deacon, each of whom prominently published on similar subjects.[285] In fact, John Layard's *The Stone Men of Malekula* (1942) was dedicated to W.H.R. Rivers.[286] Furthermore, British religious studies also utilized strongly diffusionist arguments at the time, as in the works of the presidents of the folklore society: S. H. Hooke and E. O. James.[287] It was in this diffusionistic milieu that Elliot Smith, Perry, and Rivers attempted to create a scientifically sound synthesis of the best research then available, which they thought pointed to ancient culture movements across broad spans of the globe.

---

[282] Fox, Threshold of the Pacific, 364.

[283] Ibid.

[284] Stocking, After Tylor, 293.

[285] Ibid., 301.

[286] Stocking, Functionalism Historicized, 53.

[287] Kuklick, The Savage Within, 129, n. 14.

CHAPTER SEVEN

SYNTHESIS

W. J. Perry, W. H. R. Rivers, and Grafton Elliot Smith's work on diffusion was essentially that of holistic synthesis and their resulting books were thus a broadly synthetic accretion of data from both the sciences and humanities. When considered as an outgrowth of its academic and social context, Heliolithic diffusionism was not an entirely surprising or unexpected occurrence. Elliot Smith, like many other scholars of his day, was convinced of the role of an Asiatic/Oriental influence upon the early history of Europe.[288]

As stated earlier, much of this theory emerged in the context of debates regarding the origins of agriculture and sedentary living patterns. W. J. Perry and Elliot Smith often relied on the agricultural data and studies found in the works of Professor Thomas Cherry (1861-1945) of the University of Melbourne.[289] In 1921, Cherry had noted the distinctive periodic flood of the Nile, which operated in such a way that Cherry (and others), supposed Egypt could be the original source of true agricultural practices. G. E. Smith believed it imperative to convey the, "Oriental debt of Greece to whose ancient civilization Europe became heir."[290]

---

[288] Grafton Elliot Smith, The Ancient Egyptians and Their Influence upon the Civilisation of Europe, (London: Harper and Brothers, 1923), 22-23.

[289] Ibid., 2.; W. J. Perry, The Children of the Sun, (New York: E. P. Dutton and Company, 1923), 36-289 passim.

[290] Smith, The Ancient Egyptians, 24.

However, Cherry was clearly not the sole stimuli for the British diffusionists as they cast their nets far and wide for data.

W. H. R. Rivers pointed to influential writings by Augustus Henry Lane Fox Pitt Rivers (1827-1900). A. Lane Fox, as he was sometimes called, was in turn influenced by both Herbert Spencer and Charles Darwin. The Heliolithic critique also centered on pointing out the diffusionist arguments contained in the works of Pitt Rivers and others. Though many authors of the time developed typological social evolutionist models of human development, Rivers and his colleagues became increasingly critical of the underlying dangerous assumptions of such theories. They were particularly disturbed by what they took to be the unilinear evolutionist insistence on an unvarying trajectory for certain societies that necessitated the emergence of, what was to them, the ills of civilization as it had developed over time and brought about wide-scale destructive tendencies. For the British diffusionists, social evolutionism was dependent upon assumptions which represented violence as natural and progressively developmental for humanity and that a conflict-oriented culture has been endemic as an overall component of inherent human nature.

To further our examination of pertinent sources, however, one must note that Elliot Smith made use of the thirteen volume series entitled *The Mythology of All Races* (1916-1932) edited by philologist and Orientalist Louis Herbert Gray (1875-1955). Particularly significant were the sections on Egyptian mythology contributed by diffusionist Max Muller and Stephen Henry Langdon on Semitic mythology, among others. Furthermore, Elliot Smith relied on the work of Fritz Netolitzky (1875-1945) on ancient Egyptian diets, botanical, and horticultural studies.[291] Netolitzky's

---

[291] Ibid., 48-50. Moreover, contemporary scholars were not looking for such connections in varied fields of research, thus few of them were aware of Netolitzky's work.

examinations were principally published in German and thus seem not to have been widely available in England for some time after initial release.

On a related note, the British diffusionists sought architectural information in the research of William Richard Lethaby (1857-1931), especially his *Architecture* (1912) and *Form in Civilisation* (1922). Another architect and architectural writer of note was James Fergusson (1808-1886) who had a great influence on others of his time. Fergusson's *Rude Stone Monuments in All Countries: Their Age and Uses* (1872) was, at least, suggestive of diffusion and played a part in the Heliolithic diffusionist scenario. Both Rivers and Elliot Smith noted their acceptance of some of Fergussun's analyses.[292] Rivers and G. E. Smith also looked to earlier studies that had proposed a relationship between locations of metallurgy, precious stones, and serpent cults. For this, they found ample evidence in the works of Fergusson and in A. W. Buckland's "The Serpent in Connection with Primitive Metallurgy" (1874-1878) and her 1891 *Anthropological Studies*.[293] Elliot Smith thought that key findings explicated in these works were indicative of contacts when he researched the appearance of serpent cults among the Greeks, Phoenicians, Egyptians, and a number of localities in India.[294]

Moreover, the Heliolithic school found that James H. Breasted's (1865-1935) *The Conquest of Civilization* (1926) supported a rather loose form of the diffusion of civilization. Breasted proposed a "Fertile Crescent" or Near East diffusion

---

[292] W. H. R. Rivers, Psychology and Politics: And Other Essays, (New York: Harcourt, Brace and Company, 1923), 111.

[293] Ibid.

[294] G. E. Smith, The Evolution of the Dragon, (Manchester: University of Manchester Press, 1919), 47-108.

scenario in *Ancient Times: A History of the Early World* (1916). Indeed, W. J. Perry heavily relied on the work of Breasted for information on Egypt.[295] Perry contributed to Francis Sydney Marvin's *England and the World* (1925) wherein he mentioned the wanderings of peoples and the diffusion of culture.

In much the same way, John Dunmore Lang's (1799-1878) *Origin and Migrations of the Polynesian Nation* (1834) was of notable application to both Rivers and Perry as was Georg Friederici's *Malaio-Polynesische Wanderungen* (1914), which covered some Polynesian genealogies and oral traditions. In addition, Elliot Smith relied upon other reference material culled from Alexander von Humboldt in *Vues des cordilleres et monumens des peuples indigenes de l'Amerique* (1810-1813). Von Humboldt collected information on the Americas and, though much of the work was later shown to be flawed, Elliot Smith found it useful in drawing the broad connections he believed existed between the Old World and the New.

Such flaws, as they came to sometimes be glaring in later periods, demonstrate that the work of the diffusionist school was not without significant errors. For instance, Elliot Smith's reliance on a few of the writings of and artworks by Jean-Frederic Maximilien de Waldeck (1766-1875) is unfortunate. That is because it appears that de Waldeck's drawings of Mesoamerican discoveries were skewed in favor of his boss Lord Kingsborough. De Waldeck, as Glyn Daniel has cleverly pointed out, intentionally manufactured drawings of objects and animals in the Americas to make them appear more similar to Old World works than they actually were. Kingsborough died in a debtor's prison after spending his life earnings attempting to prove that the "Lost Tribes" could be found in the Americas. It is important to note, however, that Elliot Smith was very critical of those theories and he considered them to be preposterous.

---

[295] Perry, The Children of the Sun, 464-465.

In a like manner, the Heliolithic school felt it important to critique other theories of diffusion originating on the European continent. In a series of lectures given between 1919 and 1922, W. H. R. Rivers discussed the diffusionist work of Bernard Ankermann, Friedrich Ratzel, and Fritz Graebner.[296] Rivers claimed that Austro-German diffusionism and British diffusionism had emerged entirely independently and with different philosophical implications and were based upon different epistemological presuppositions.[297] In contrast, Rivers also mentioned the Polynesian studies of John Macmillan Brown (1846-1935) in connection with his own and compared them favorably. Rivers was eminently concerned with Brown's *Maori and Polynesian* (1907).[298] Brown explicated his own interpretation of a migration of peoples into the Polynesian island by way of overseas routes that originated in Asian mainlands and related to cultural developments in Indonesia, all of which were critiqued by Rivers during his lecture period.[299]

During the 1919-1922 lectures, Rivers also commented that geographer Ellsworth Huntington (1876-1947) had proposed ideas suggestive of a mechanism for cultural change as related to population movements.[300] In *The Pulse of Asia* (1907), Huntington began to develop a geographical-climatic theory that suggested great changes in climate lead to migration and shifted the 'centre of

---

[296] Rivers, Psychology and Politics, 114-115.

[297] Ibid.

[298] Ibid., 119.

[299] John Macmillan Brown, Maori and Polynesian: Their Origin, History and Culture, (London: Hutchinson and Company, 1907), 2-37 passim.

[300] Rivers, Psychology and Politics, 120-124.

civilisation', yet this did not mean that Rivers subscribed to a climatic determinism of culture change.[301] Rivers was, however, convinced that the work of Charles Gabriel Seligman (1873-1940) and Thomas Athol Joyce (1878-1942) related to his own increasingly diffusionist perspective.[302] C. G. Seligman, a friend of Rivers, was also a member of the foundational Cambridge 1898 expedition to Torres Straits and later a moderate diffusionist in his own right. Subsequently, T. A. Joyce contributed to ethnology, museums, and Central American and West Indian archeology.

Lastly, Rivers much like Smith was also aware of the Heliolithic school's cumulative shortcomings. For example, he pointed out that despite his long investigation into the subject, there were a series of remaining questions: what was the original home of the traversing groups, what was their ethnicity, and, most importantly, what were the dates involved?[303] For these Rivers knew there were no easy answers and that these problems stood in the way of any broad acceptance of diffusionism.

Diffusionist Paleontology

In relation to the 'Peking Man' finds of his former student Davidson Black, Swedish archeologist and geologist Johan Gunnar Andersson (1874-1960) suggested in 1921 that fossil human finds would be made in China near Choukoutien (Zoukoudian), which did occur. What is important here is that Andersson's work must also be seen in light of the diffusionist work of Oscar Montelius. In

---

[301] Ellsworth Huntington, The Pulse of Asia: A Journey in Central Asia Illuminating the Geographic Basis of History, (London: Archibald Constable and Company, 1907), 35.

[302] Rivers, Psychology and Politics, 124.

[303] Ibid., 125.

1934 Kegan Paul, Trench, Trubner, publisher of a number of the Heliolithic school's books, released Andersson's *Children of the Yellow Earth: Studies in Prehistoric China*. Andersson was the curator of the Museum of Far Eastern Antiquities in Sweden and made several expeditions to northern and northwest China—he often considered the role of diffusion in archeological distributions.

Many comparable discoveries were made during this time based upon diffusionist assumptions. For example, in 1931, at Edinburgh University, Elliot Smith presented a lecture discussing the work of W. C. Pei at Choukoutien, Davidson Black, and Teilhard de Chardin.[304] G. E. Smith's tangential relationship to the important discoveries made in China was of great import to him and, he believed, these findings supported his notions of how early extraordinary human population movements were possible. This viewpoint of the past caused Smith to regard all of humanity as intricately connected over a vast timescale that others were still struggling to come to grasp.

Because of these populational convictions Elliot Smith openly repudiated racist concepts writing, "Using the term in a strictly biological sense, all peoples living on the earth are members of one and the same species…we are bound to admit that all belong to the same zoological species."[305] In addition, Rivers joined Elliot Smith in his scorn of so-called race differences—in fact, Rivers went through his career "virtually never using the word 'race' himself."[306]

---

[304] Grafton Elliot Smith, The Significance of the Peking Man, (Edinburgh: The Henderson Trust, 1931), 5-20.

[305] Grafton Elliot Smith, Human History, (London: Cape, 1934), 55-56.

[306] Graham D. Richards, "William Halse Rivers (1864-1922)," *The Psychologist* 14, no. 9 (September 2001): 464.

Elliot Smith further stressed that other anthropologists should refrain from confusing cultural traits with race.[307]

In 1935 G. E. Smith condemned, "those who, taking advantage of the glamour of the Darwinian doctrine, talked nonsense in the name of anthropological science."[308] Elliot Smith's critique also extended to the earlier biblical catastrophists.[309] In this connection, he praised the diligent efforts of Jacques Boucher de Crevecoeur de Perthes (1788-1868) and his attempts to undermine both the diluvialist and catastrophist claims of human creation in the precise year of 4004 BCE.[310] G. E. Smith also looked favorably upon the comparativist work of William Johnson Sollas (1849-1936) of Oxford, who contributed to anthropology, geology, and zoology.[311] Much in the same way as Elliot Smith, Sollas believed in establishing a broader connection between all fields of knowledge—the sciences in particular. Moreover, both underscored the significance of diffusion to early paleontology.

India and Politics

To further demonstrate that the diffusionists were great synthesizers and relied upon the leaders of academia in their time,

---

[307] Grafton Elliot Smith, Elephants and Ethnologists, (New York: E. P. Dutton and Company, 1924), 104.

[308] Grafton Elliot Smith, The Place of Thomas Henry Huxley in Anthropology—The Huxley Memorial Lecture for 1935, (London: Royal Anthropological Institute of Great Britain and Ireland, 1935), 5.

[309] Smith, Human History, 68-69.

[310] Ibid., 70.

[311] Ibid., 98. One of Sollas' top accomplishments was to add to the sense of the great age of the planet.

Perry quoted from the works of Robert Bruce Foote (1834-1912) for data on the prehistory of India.[312] Foote, a British archeologist and geologist, was among the founders of Indian prehistory. There is also evidence that Rivers, towards the end of his life, had become increasingly focused on archeological and ethnological developments in India.[313] Rivers' heightened interest in India is demonstrated in a large section of the posthumously released *Social Organization* (1924).[314] These and related interests helped establish the intellectual roots for the British diffusionists.

There were also a number other philosophical and intellectual roots to the beliefs of the diffusionists. For example, Elliot Smith sometimes noted that he was philosophically opposed to and highly critical of the theories of Thomas Hobbes on human nature.[315] In fact, he considered Hobbesian theory selfish and inordinately anti-social.[316] These ideas were reflected in G. E. Smith's disapproval of Conservative Prime Minister Stanley Baldwin (1867-1947), who was infamous for his strong anti-labor position and the 1927 Trade Disputes Act.[317] Elliot Smith was also disgusted with the views of Labour/National Prime Minister James Ramsay MacDonald (1866-1937), David Lloyd George (1863-1945), and especially Robert Cecil (1864-1958). This supports a conclusion that there was a strong political aspect to the

---

[312] Perry, The Children of the Sun, 47.

[313] W. H. R. Rivers, Social Organization, with a preface by G. E. Smith, edited by W. J. Perry, (New York: Alfred A. Knopf, Inc., 1924), 141-158.

[314] Ibid.

[315] Smith, Human History, 171.

[316] Ibid., 172.

[317] Ibid., 175.

diffusionist's beliefs. The Heliolithic school's works can be seen as philosophically unified, not only on the issue of culture diffusion but also on more thoroughly political issues with which they were experiencing at the time.

In line with the synthesis approach of Elliot Smith, from around 1910, Rivers "had been keenly advancing a view of the human sciences as facets of a single overarching project" with a loose political aim.[318] University of Staffordshire psychology historian Graham D. Richards has gone so far as to explicitly state that Rivers' writings were "highly sane".[319] This is in contradistinction to some of the implied arguments of the Heliolithic school's critics, who often subtly (and sometimes overtly) assert that the group did not making rational arguments.

G. E. Smith's *Human History* embodied many of his diffusionist, philosophical, and political theories in this culminatory work. Elliot Smith held to the innate goodness of human nature and 'Natural Man'.[320] In this, Elliot Smith rejected racist culture theory when he wrote, "Any member of any race can adopt the culture of another people without undergoing any change in his physical characteristics."[321] His opposition to Hobbesian and evolutionist ideas was because, for him, malice and envy stemmed from artificiality. As a result, "It must not be forgotten that warfare and cruelty, injustice and brutality are equally the results of civilisation and are not natural modes of behaviour."[322] He praised 'the

---

[318] Richards, "William Halse Rivers (1864-1922)," 464.

[319] Ibid.

[320] Smith, Human History, 53-54.

[321] Ibid., 131.

[322] Ibid., 173-174.

Arcadian manner of living', and was appalled at statements from political leaders that assumed an aggressive and warlike nature to be inherent to humankind.[323] One example was Viscount Chelwood's speech in the first Rickman Godlee Lecture entitled *The Cooperation of Nations* (UCL, 1927). Chelwood claimed that increased organization from clans to tribes to states decreased conflict and barbarism. G. E. Smith called this presentation an "imaginary picture of life among savages."[324] In contrast, Elliot Smith praised President Calvin Coolidge's Armistice Address of November 1928 in which the natural goodness of humanity was extolled upon and wherein it was suggested that massive warfare was to be only temporary.[325] Thus, much of the Heliolithic approach appears to have been underpinned with moral issues in relation to the interpretation of the human past.

Elliot Smith went on to note that Aristotle, Baruch Spinoza, Thomas More, and Desiderius Erasmus had all acknowledged the peacefulness of foreigners but after John Locke, it became common to ignore man's natural morality.[326] G. E. Smith realized the experiential *tabula rasa* was damaging to the concept of innate moral principles—though he did accept the variability of experience, he felt that Locke had simply went too far.[327] Smith believed that he had discovered the physico-anatomical or bio-neurological basis for self-preservation that entailed an avoidance of conflict. He referred to it as an "intuitive natural impulse to decent behaviour" which

---

[323] Ibid., 174-175.

[324] Ibid., 175.

[325] Ibid.

[326] Ibid., 170-178.

[327] Ibid., 178.

could only be overridden by powerful social processes and artificialities grafted into human culture.[328] Consequently, he thought that philosophers such as Hume were unscientific and too speculative because they made a number of unfounded assumptions and, ultimately, ignored direct observational evidence. Since they were unaware of the facts, Elliot Smith claimed, they were only capable of espousing opinions.[329] His own study of the facts suggested to him that civilization itself inherently entailed a number of moral quandaries which compelled the behavior of peoples in limited directions.

Elliot Smith claimed that one could only find "the real character of mankind when free from the complications and embarrassments of civilisation."[330] Elliot Smith was pleased with the 'Arcadian simplicity' that existed before the unnatural artificialities of civilization had emerged.[331] G. E. Smith referred to these ancient human groups as having "no social organization," by which he meant: no class divisions, no differentiation of rank (hierarchical divisions), and broad social equality or egalitarianism. He found sedentary, settled, and village life all unnatural—only family (bands), nomadism, and significant sprawling domain areas were natural over the broadest sense of human existence.[332] Smith said that the "artificial aims" of civilization only cause "rivalry and jealousy" and, instead, humankind should return to an earlier form

---

[328] Ibid., 179.

[329] Ibid., 180.

[330] Ibid., 232.

[331] Ibid., 233.

[332] Ibid., 235.

of social arrangement and embrace the good that is found within such limited organization.[333]

Elliot Smith believed that the original and natural state of human organization to be closely analogous to that observed among the anthropoid apes.[334] He also declared that the psychological and sociological concepts of the 'herd instinct' and 'primal horde' discussed respectively by J. J. Atkinson in *Primal Law* (1903) and Freud's *Totem and Taboo* (1919), to be "fictions pure and simple and the ethnological theories based upon it are illusory."[335] According to Elliot Smith and W. J. Perry, there was no accumulation of property amongst early humans until "contaminated" by sedentary agriculture and civilization.[336] Such beliefs prompted the Heliolithic diffusionists to develop elaborate theories of the many fields of human knowledge, all of which attempted to first locate a biological basis and then a sociological basis for the origins of such beliefs and practices.

Elliot Smith, much like Rivers, desired to merge the sciences and the humanities into a "unified discipline" or "a science of history", yet carefully pointed out human behavior does not fit neatly into any 'laws of nature'. Elliot Smith presented what he called "a new synthesis."[337] This new synthesis was to be built philosophically upon observation and inductive methodology.[338]

---

[333] Ibid., 236.

[334] Ibid., 235-237.

[335] Ibid., 236.

[336] Ibid., 239.

[337] Ibid., xiii.

[338] Ibid., xiv.

For inspiration, he pointed to the efforts of Andreas Vesalius (1514-1564) and Copernicus and hailed Galileo and Darwin, all of whom undermined what he called the 'tyranny of tradition' represented in the works of Galen, Ptolemy, and Aristotle.[339]

Altogether, according to Elliot Smith, the attainment, preservation, and continuity of life were the central concerns of humans.[340] Humanity's collective efforts to preserve their lives led to the creation of civilization yet brought with it many unanticipated consequences.[341] W. H. R. Rivers appeared to have agreed with this assertion.[342] Elliot Smith claimed that unquestioned 'ancient authority' hindered progress and stated that though Francis Bacon (1561-1626) and Descartes had made tremendous intellectual contributions, they became the new authorities placed beyond question which had had a stultifying effect on scientists.[343] He ultimately noted that 'Newtonian discipline' and "the stinging whip of Voltaire" broke some of Cartesianism's sway.[344] As the concepts were to further develop, the theories of Smith, Rivers, and Perry, at times received broad distribution through their attainment of funding and access to outlets for publication.

---

[339] Ibid., 21.

[340] Ibid., 6-7.

[341] Ibid., 14-15.

[342] W. H. R. Rivers, in G. E. Smith, ed., <u>Medicine, Magic and Religion: The FitzPatrick Lectures Delivered Before the Royal College of Physicians of London 1915 and 1916</u>, (New York: Harcourt, Brace and Company, 1924), 127-130.

[343] Smith, <u>Human History</u>, 19.

[344] Ibid., 21.

CHAPTER EIGHT

FUNDING AND CONCLUSION

Methuen and Kegan Paul published many of Elliot Smith, Perry, and Rivers' books. Over half of all books released during this period by Kegan Paul were self-published, yet that was not the case for the Heliolithic school of thought.[345] Kegan Paul combined in 1889 with Nicholas Trubner's group which often published on subjects of the East and works by Orientalists.[346] It can be argued that Kegan Paul was an outlet for proponents of scientific rationalism, an approach that was plainly obvious throughout the publications of Rivers, Perry, and Elliot Smith. Together, their publishing ventures helped to undermine what were to their view outdated scientific assumptions of Victorian academicians. Access to publishers was a major boost to the diffusionists, which was only surpassed by the impact of the impressive early funding they received from major foundations.

The University College, London had two-thirds of its medical department buildings paid for by Carnegie and Rockefeller donations.[347] Elliot Smith chose the chair at UCL over Cambridge because he considered it to be a challenge that he welcomed. Once

---

[345] Jonathan R. Rose and Patricia J. Anderson, eds., British Literary Publishing Houses, 1820-1880, (Detroit: Gale Research: 1991), 3-32; Leslie Howsam, Kegan Paul—A Victorian Imprint: Publishers, Books and Cultural History, (Toronto: University of Toronto Press, 1998), 118-200 passim.

[346] Ibid.

[347] Warren Royal Dawson, ed., Sir Grafton Elliot Smith: A Biographical Record by His Colleagues, (London: Jonathan Cape, 1938), 171-172. These areas were damaged significantly during World War II.

he accepted the position, Smith proceeded to coax from the Rockefeller Foundation "the largest single benefaction to any educational institution in Great Britain."[348] From about 1920 to 1925/6, G. E. Smith received incredible Rockefeller support.[349] In fact, in 1920 Elliot Smith was the principle beneficiary of a massive five million dollar grant to UCL, mainly for the Department of Anatomy.[350] By 1938, the four Rockefeller philanthropies had given some 2.4 million dollars to anthropology alone.[351] However, great changes were to occur that affected the diffusionist's chances to further research, elaborate, and teach their interpretive framework.

A vast reorganization of the Rockefeller Foundation took place in 1928. According to Raymond D. Fosdick, who recounted the history of the Foundation in 1952, the foundation beginnings marked a great new era of philanthropy as it quickly emerged.[352] The Rockefeller Foundation had funded UCL diffusionist anthropologists well into the late 1920s, but suddenly cut all funding

---

[348] Ibid., 173.

[349] Henrika Kuklick, The Savage Within: The Social History of British Anthropology, 1885-1945, (New York: Cambridge University Press, 1992), 210-211.

[350] George W. Stocking, Jr., ed., "Philanthropoids and Vanishing Cultures: Rockefeller Funding and the End of the Museum Era in Anglo-American Anthropology," in Objects and Others: Essays on Museums and Material Culture, (Madison, Wisconsin: The University of Wisconsin Press, 1985), 118.

[351] Ibid., 116-133 passim.

[352] Michael A. Cremo and Richard L. Thompson, Forbidden Archeology: The Hidden History of the Human Race, (Los Angeles: Bhaktivedanta Book Publishing, 1998), 538, 140.

and support for social anthropology at that institution thereby shifting support to the London School of Economics (LSE) functionalists.[353] According to Kuklick, "The triumph of functionalism in British anthropology…was a consequence of the support its practitioners received from the Rockefeller Foundation's donations to the LSE and the [International African Institute] IAI."[354]

Given that the Rockefeller Foundation made a staggering donation in 1920 to the UCL, the assumption was that the university would develop into a veritable pipeline of diffusion-oriented scholars who would then go on to major positions within academia.[355] However, by 1927-1928 the major ground shift within the Rockefeller Foundation took place and the changeover in funding moved from Grafton Elliot Smith to the structural-functionalist oriented LSE.[356] Kuklick contends that Malinowski and the Rockefeller Foundation allied with the Rhodes House at Oxford to support the structural-functionalist paradigm due to Malinowski repeatedly communicating with them and successfully convincing the parties concerned that his methodology had more to offer in the long run.[357] UCL graduates of a diffusionary allegiance were then essentially shut out of professorships in Britain as most posts went to LSE graduates.[358] Effectively, this meant that, "those

---

[353] Kuklick, The Savage Within, 63.

[354] Ibid., 212.

[355] Ibid., 394.

[356] Ibid., 398.

[357] Ibid., 400-401.

[358] Ibid., 55.

persons trained at the LSE exercised near-monopolistic control of post-World War II anthropology."[359] Regardless, the British diffusionists were not consigned to total defeat.

Elliot Smith attempted to attain further funding for UCL anthropological research in 1926 and 1927 but failed to garner a positive response.[360] There was also a bigger conflict between the competing universities across Britain, specifically the LSE and UCL which appears to have played some role in the decision-making process.[361] Ultimately, in February 1927, all funding was denied except for UCL's Department of Anatomy, which was provided primarily because of Elliot Smith's renowned stature more or less the preeminent personage in this field.[362] The decline from this period, though, was precipitous.

Between 1927 and 1930, Grafton Elliot Smith lost virtually all of the support of the Rockefeller Foundation.[363] Following the aforementioned 1928 reorganization of the Rockefeller Foundation, structural-functionalism was ascendant.[364] The Rockefeller Foundation's commitment to Malinowski and the International African Institute was complete.[365] These events served as a stimulus

---

[359] Ibid., 56.

[360] Ian Langham, The Building of British Social Anthropology: W. H. R. Rivers and His Cambridge Disciples in the Development of Kinship Studies, 1989-1931, (Boston, Mass.: D. Reidel, 1981), 182-183.

[361] Ibid., 184-185.

[362] Ibid., 185.

[363] Stocking, Objects and Others, 124-125.

[364] Ibid., 125.

for the diffusion of structural-functionalism to many future professorships, students, and the histories written of the discipline. In the fall of 1932, Radcliffe-Brown and Malinowski worked together in a concerted effort to win additional funding from the tax-exempt foundations.[366] Their combined influence met with roaring success. A. R. Radcliffe-Brown was at the University of Chicago until 1937, and then moved on for the rest of his career to Oxford. By 1938, Malinowski was in some ways surpassed by Radcliffe-Brown, who was the Royal Anthropological Institute (RAI) president in 1940 and 1941.[367]

Plainly, as George Stocking, Jr. wrote, the philanthropist's "prejudice in favor of Malinowski surely contributed to his rise at the expense of the diffusionists at University College."[368] In further moves away from the historicist and diffusionist approaches, "The pattern of Rockefeller institutional support reflected this: the…[LSE] was supported at the expense of Elliot Smith's University College."[369] However, there were contradictory elements of both a loss in prominence but somehow sustaining a position of academic prominence. For example, in 1922 Grafton Elliot Smith was commissioned by *Encyclopedia Britannica* to provide the entry 'Anthropology', which was retained all the way until the 1926 edition.[370]

---

[365] George Stocking, Jr., <u>After Tylor: British Social Anthropology, 1888-1951</u>, (Madison, Wisconsin: University of Wisconsin Press, 1995), 408.

[366] Ibid., 403.

[367] Ibid., 366.

[368] Stocking, <u>Objects and Others</u>, 134.

[369] Ibid., 139-140. In general, Carnegie money funded archeology and physical anthropology while biology and ethnography were Rockefeller funded.

Despite this tentative acceptance only a combination of issues could lead to the demise of Heliolithic diffusionism and the opportunity for self-correction be denied. Recent scholarship has portrayed the changes within the field as one decided purely upon facts and data, rather than examining the socio-economic aspects of what took place. For instance, Alan Barnard has written in an assessment with which the present author does not entirely agree, "Ultimately, the scientific advances in archaeology in the 1940s proved beyond doubt that the Egypt of 4000 BC could not have been the source of all human culture."[371] As historian of anthropology George Stocking, Jr. has pointed out, by 1951, social anthropology was the prevailing method of study within the discipline (and primarily in the form of the structural-functional paradigm).[372] Typical of a modernist presentation, in his otherwise tremendous history of archeology, Bruce Trigger wrote, "In the United Kingdom ethnologists rejected the sterile diffusionism of Elliot Smith and his followers by adopting the structural-functionalist approach."[373] Paul A. Erickson and Liam D. Murphy have stated that Heliolithic diffusionism's demise may be partially attributed to World War II and the rejection of diffusionistic schemas in general due to a perceived relation with racialist ideology

---

[370] Langham, The Building of British Social Anthropology, 171. In addition, in 1926, W. J. Perry joined the RAI council.

[371] Alan Barnard, History and Theory in Anthropology, (New York: Cambridge University Press, 2000), 53.

[372] Stocking, After Tylor, 431.

[373] Bruce Trigger, A History of Archaeological Thought, (New York: Cambridge University Press, 1989), 245.

which, as noted in previous chapters, would be a fallacious connection when it comes to G. E. Smith, Perry, and Rivers.[374]

There should also be some consideration of anthropologist Fred Voget's reason for the demise of the diffusionist theory when he wrote, "In the absence of clear documentation, culture historicists substituted formal analysis and classification for process."[375] But Voget made it evident he had not understood the primary source material in his critique 'Culture Historicism: An Assessment' when he surmised, "Such a model presupposed a uniform rate of diffusion for all traits, regardless of kind, and posed no barrier to transmission other than mountain ranges and large bodies of water."[376] This form of misunderstanding has been typical of those not relying on a large number of primary sources. In the bibliographies of many of these histories, the authors list no more than a handful of diffusionist books and, oftentimes, not the texts representative of the final development of the Heliolithic theory.

The processes of change in the field of anthropology were part of a not simply ahistorical but an antihistorical turn by the structural-functionalists.[377] The development of internalist approaches to culture change received increased impetus from Willard Libby's invention of radiocarbon (C-14) dating

---

[374] Paul Erickson and Liam Murphy, eds., A History of Anthropological Theory, (Orchard Park, New York: Broadview Press, 1998), 55.

[375] Fred Voget, A History of Ethnology, (New York: Holt, Rinehart and Winston, 1975), 355.

[376] Ibid.

[377] George Stocking, Jr., Functionalism Historicized: Essays on British Social Anthropology, (Madison, Wisconsin: University of Wisconsin Press, 1984), v. 2, 115.

techniques.[378] This allowed for elaborate and near universal (or globally applicable) dating as opposed to the previous relative dating methods. And, as noted by Trigger, "By greatly slowing the rate of cultural change…radiocarbon dating made it easier for archaeologists to credit the possibility that major changes had come about as a result of internal changes rather than attributing them to diffusion and migration as they previously had done."[379]

There was also the matter of the use of different scholarly languages that caused problems. This was related to the perceived, and real, conflicts between Classics, Egyptology, and anthropology. Many perceived a 'relative loss' of world power by Britain and increased nationalistic/imperialistic tendencies which directed socio-political aspects of society that concomitantly included academia.[380] Through Malinowski's efforts, "In alliance with colonial policy makers he elicited patronage for the International African Institute, which became a mechanism for the dispersal of funds to functionalist anthropologists—who thereby assumed dominance of their discipline." In fact, in an unfortunate formulation, "unlikely alliances were formed among anthropologists, colonial policy makers, and philanthropists."[381]

---

[378] Trigger, <u>A History of Anthropological Thought</u>, 304.

[379] Ibid., 305. Radiocarbon dating brought about the greatest problems for the Heliolithic approach and nearly reversed the direction from great advancements made in stone architecture from an east to west direction, to a west to east movement. Some have speculated Rivers, Elliot Smith, and Perry would have preferred to reverse the direction of movement in their own time but never had the evidence to support such claims. The present author, however, tends to doubt such an assertion.

[380] Ibid., 257, 262, 278.

[381] Ibid., 182.

Colonial regimes were intrigued by structural-functionalism because it seemed to adhere to their aims of applicable, practical, and utilitarian science.[382] It was seen by such regimes as amenable to social engineering and the reorganization of colonial and post-colonial societies. In point of fact, Malinowski agreed, "that functionalist theories and findings were more serviceable in the colonial context."[383] As Trigger has eloquently pointed out, "But the functionalists were then able to strike a responsive chord in official hearts because they echoed ideological refrains long dear to colonial rulers."[384] Additionally, regarding the Rockefeller Foundation funding of the LSE, "This decision literally favored the younger generation."[385]

Malinowski gathered an influential group of scholars and "founded a tight professional organization"—the Association of Social Anthropologists (ASA) in 1946, much of the work that they performed in common was for the IAI.[386] Along with the Social Science Research Council (SSRC), much of the funding from 1924 on went to these two organizations.[387] The LSE became the main beneficiary of the Foundation, receiving several million dollars from 1923 to 1939, with Radcliffe-Brown and Malinowski being the principle recipients.[388] This was partially because they met the

---

[382] Ibid., 186.

[383] Ibid.

[384] Ibid., 182.

[385] Ibid., 63.

[386] Jack Goody, <u>The Expansive Moment: Anthropology in Britain and Africa, 1917-1970</u>, (New York: Cambridge University Press, 1995), 1-2.

[387] Ibid., 2.

Foundation's presentist and practicality oriented funding focus at that time which had little interest in an anthropological approach attempting to determine the historical beginnings for populations and any subsequent movements.[388] Between 1937 and 1951, Malinowski and Radcliffe-Brown's students took control of the top academic positions from Oxford to Manchester to Cambridge and even a few positions in the Americas.

More than this, the donations from other organizations were provided in support of a unified ideology. [390] As Kuklick pointed out, "Like the Rockefeller Foundation, the Carnegie Corporation saw its role as assisting the British colonial regimes to govern more efficiently."[391] Therefore, the support for the RAI between 1924 and 1930 was significant.[392] Yet, the RAI was, for Malinowski, too tolerant of differing anthropological views and under his urging, the Rockefeller Foundation cut funding heavily to any other interpretations that meandered to far afield for the utilitarian demands of practicality.[393] Consequently, the organization's aims "to be an independent, impartial agency" were curtailed and yet another blow was dealt to the British diffusionists.[394]

---

[388] Ibid., 13-14, 25.

[389] Ibid., 20.

[390] Ibid., 144.

[391] Kuklick, The Savage Within, 215.

[392] Ibid., 211.

[393] Ibid., 211-212, n. 85 and n. 86.

[394] Ibid., 210. This is not to suggest that Malinowski had a malevolent intent, because he truly seemed to believe that he had the correct interpretive framework.

In the end, together Malinowski and Radcliffe-Brown had brought about the synchronic presentist view as opposed to the diachronic historicist approach for anthropologists.[395] Such an outlook was precisely that desired by colonialists and the new power brokers in anthropology. As James Urry noted, "Patronage, nepotism and the control of access to grants, publication and academic posts were as important in shaping British anthropology as they often were in other academic disciplines, perhaps more so given its extremely small membership."[396]

CONCLUSION

The academic debate between independent invention and diffusion operated in a nexus between the fall of unilinear social evolutionism as a paradigm and the triumph of structural-functionalism and involved a crucial conflict between diachronic and synchronic interpretations in anthropology. The structural-functionalism of Malinowski and Radcliffe-Brown was, however, to retain elements of social evolutionism and a preference for independent invention. The historical representations of the controversy often mask the root differences in the theoretical viewpoints of independent invention and diffusion. These viewpoints represented a conflict, as pointed out by George

---

[395] Hans F. Vermeulen and Arturo Alvarez Roldan, eds. Fieldwork and Footnotes: Studies in the History of European Anthropology, (New York: Routledge, 1995), 147. Diachronic: seeks to understand changes over time as interpreted by social evolutionists and diffusionists. Synchronic: seeks to explain the present in terms of the present, according to the structural-functionalists.

[396] James Urry, Before Social Anthropology: Essays on the History of British Social Anthropology, (Reading: Harwood Academic Publishers, 1993), 16, n. 10.

Stocking, Jr., between synchronic and diachronic analysis.[397] Synchronic analysis represented a static interpretation of culture (being presentist) rather than diffusionism's dynamic interpretation of cultural development and spread (being historicist). The diffusionist's were also somewhat out of sync with the broader paradigm of anthropological thought as it was experiencing a greater influence from the subdiscipline of archeology.[398]

The academic trend at the time tended to favor practical (or useful) and utilitarian studies. Applicable studies were also appreciated by the Rockefeller Foundation and its various trusts, which donated incredible largesse to academic institutions that were just becoming established fields and experiencing increased institutionalization, professionalization, and specialization as the markers of true science. Moreover, the work of Malinowski held within it a number of assumptions from previous ethnological models oft-decried by the British diffusionists. These assumptions included strong biases toward deterministic interpretations of cultural practices.

Among the provisional conclusions that may be drawn regarding this period of anthropology, would be that the diffusionist school emerged principally due to the lack of an entrenched paradigmatic opposition and was eventually refuted through a number of field discoveries, dating discrepancies, and alterations in funding. The contributions of the diffusionists and other related developments, however, had positive effects such as creating an increased interest in Egyptian culture in and of itself, perhaps leading to some level of real appreciation of Africa and African

---

[397] Stocking, After Tylor, 301-388 passim.

[398] If you prefer to refer to archeology as one of the four primary fields of anthropology (as Americanists today typically classify it) that would also be applicable here rather than the term 'subdiscipline' which some may find offensive.

cultures. Although potentially productive research agendas were abandoned in favor of the structural-functionalist venues, the diffusion debates forced the field of anthropology to take definitive positions on the issue of culture analysis and description and created an opportunity for clarification of the parameters of acceptable scientific anthropological research. The British diffusionists also helped to increase the emerging critique of racialist and typological thought.

Finally, it is plausible that some of the cultural diffusionist theories deserve closer inspection rather than being discounted based upon modern presuppositions based upon a lack of primary historical source research. The reductionist approach of the structural-functionalists worked to obscure the more generally holistic approach, findings, and methodology as developed within British diffusionism. The rejection of the diffusionist approach further appears to have been based upon misunderstandings regarding the scope of their claims, modern anthropologist's perhaps unintentional misrepresentation of the diffusionist's historical context, and overly-critical assumptions that all diffusionism bears an implicit relationship with racialist beliefs since the same argument could be turned against isolationists. These elements, joined with a lack of reference to all of the most relevant primary sources and a heavy reliance on purely critical secondary sources, has created a problem wherein modern anthropology has abandoned or vehemently decries or ignores all aspects of British diffusionism, along with any possible fruitful areas of anthropological research related to such an approach.

Ultimately, these problems, combined with the proponents' passing in 1922 (Rivers), 1937 (Smith), and 1949 (Perry), respectively, to play a significant part in the demise of the opportunity for cultural diffusionism to contribute a greater amount of research in anthropology. As Martin Bernal wrote about the demise of the Heliolithic school, "Nevertheless, the threat to anthropology that Elliot Smith represented at a vulnerable stage in the discipline's development can still be seen: it is in the shudder or grimace at the mention of his name or the word 'diffusionism' that is still a necessary sign of orthodoxy or 'competence' in the field."[399]

---

[399] Martin Bernal, <u>Black Athena: The Afroasiatic Roots of Classical Civilization,</u> (New Brunswick, New Jersey: Rutgers University Press, 2003), v. I, 272. This is a pertinent reference to conservative orthodox interpretations of anthropology which some seem to think is a badge of honor rather than an example of a closed mind.

Bibliography

Primary Sources

Boas, Franz. *Race, Language and Culture.* New York: The Macmillan Company, 1949.

Brown, John Macmillan. *Maori and Polynesian: Their Origin, History and Culture.* London: Hutchinson and Company, 1907.

Childe, Vere Gordon. *The Danube in Prehistory.* Oxford: Clarendon Press, 1929.

--------. *The Dawn of European Civilisation.* New York: Alfred A. Knopf, 1956.

--------. *A New Light on the Ancient Middle East.* New York: Alfred A. Knopf, 1958.

Codrington, Robert Henry. *The Melanesians.* Oxford: Clarendon Press, 1891.

Dawson, Warren R., Ed. *Sir Grafton Elliot Smith: A Biographical Record by His Colleagues.* London: Cape, 1938.

Dixon, Roland Burrage. *The Building of Cultures.* New York: Charles Scribner's Sons, 1928.

Elkin, Adolphus Peter, and N.W.G. Macintosh, Eds. *Grafton Elliot Smith: The Man and His Work.* Portland, Oregon: International Scholarly Book Services, 1974.

Gladwin, Harold Sterling. *Men Out of Asia*. New York: Whittlesey House, 1947.

Graebner, Fritz. *The Method of Ethnology*. Heidelberg: C. Winter, 1911.

Haddon, Alfred Cort. *A History of Anthropology*. New York: Putnam, 1910.

--------. *The Study of Man*. London: J. Murray, 1908.

--------. *The Wanderings of Peoples*. Cambridge: Cambridge University Press, 1927.

Herskovits, Melville J. *Acculturation—The Study of Culture Contact*. Gloucester, Mass.: Peter Smith, 1958.

--------. *Cultural Dynamics*. New York: Alfred A. Knopf, 1964.

--------. *Franz Boas: The Science of Man in the Making*. Clifton, New Jersey: A. M. Kelley, 1973.

Hocart, A.M. *Social Origins*. Great Britain: Richard Clay and Company Ltd., C.A. Watts and Co. Ltd., 1954.

Howells, William White. *Back of History—The Story of Our Own Origins*. Garden City, New York: Country Life Press, Doubleday and Company Inc., 1954.

Huntington, Ellsworth. *The Pulse of Asia: A Journey in Central Asia Illuminating the Geographic Basis of History*. London: Archibald Constable and Company, 1907.

Jacobs, Melville. *Pattern in Cultural Anthropology.* Homewood, Ill.: Dorsey Press, 1964.

Keesing, Felix Maxwell. *Culture Change—An Analysis and Bibliography of Anthropological Sources to 1952.* Stanford, California: Stanford University Press, 1953.

Kroeber, Alfred Louis. *Anthropology.* New York: Harcourt, Brace and World, Inc., 1948.

Linton, Ralph. *The Study of Man: An Introduction.* New York: D. Appleton-Century Company, Inc., 1936.

--------. *The Tree of Culture.* New York: Alfred A. Knopf, 1964.

Maitland, Frederic William. *A Historical Sketch of Liberty and Equality, as Ideals of English Political Philosophy from the Time of Hobbes to the Time of Coleridge.* Indianapolis: Liberty Fund, 2000.

Malinowski, Bronislaw. *Argonauts of the Western Pacific: An Account of Native Enterprise and Adventure in the Archipelagoes of Melanesian New Guinea.* New York: E. P. Dutton, 1922.

Perry, W.J. *The Children of the Sun.* New York: E. P. Dutton and Company, 1923.

--------. *The Origin of Magic and Religion.* London: Methuen Publishing, 1923.

--------. *The Primordial Ocean.* London: Methuen Publishing, 1935.

--------. Ed. *Social Organization*. London: Paul, Trench, and Trubner, 1924.

--------. "The Geographical Distribution of Terraced Cultivation and Irrigation," *Memoires and Proceedings of the Manchester Literary and Philosophical Society*. 1916.

--------. "Gods and Men". *The American Anthropologist*, 32: 165-168, 1930.

--------. "The Relationship between the Geographical Distribution of Megalithic Monuments and Ancient Mines," *Memoires and Proceedings of the Manchester Literary and Philosophical Society*, 1915.

Petrie, William Matthew Flinders. *A History of Egypt*. New York: Charles Scribner's Sons, 1899.

Raglan, Fitzroy Richard Somerset. *How Came Civilization?*. London: Methuen and Co. Ltd., 1939.

Ratzel, Friedrich. *The History of Mankind*. Translated by A. J. Butler. volumes I-III. London: Macmillan, 1896-1898.

Rivers, W. H. R. *Conflict and Dream*. London: Kegan Paul, Trench, Trubner, 1923.

--------. *The History of Melanesian Society*. volumes I-II. Cambridge: Cambridge University Press, 1914.

--------. *Instinct and the Unconscious: A Contribution to a Biological Theory of the Psycho-neuroses*. Cambridge: Cambridge

University Press, 1922.

--------. *Kinship and Social Organization*. London: Constable, 1914.

--------. *Medicine, Magic and Religion: The FitzPatrick Lectures Delivered Before the Royal College of Physicians of London 1915 and 1916*. New York: Harcourt, Brace and Company, 1924.

--------. *The Principles of Social Organization*. New York: A. A. Knopf, 1924.

--------. *Psychology and Ethnology*. New York: Harcourt, Brace and Company, 1926.

--------. *Psychology and Politics: And Other Essays*. New York: Harcourt, Brace and Company, 1923.

--------. *Social Organization*. W. J. Perry, Ed. London: Kegan Paul, Trench, Trubner, 1924.

--------. *The Todas*. New York: Macmillan, 1906.

--------. "Anthropological Research outside America". In *Reports on the Present Condition and Future Needs of the Science of Anthropology*. Publication no. 200. Washington, D. C.: Gibson Brothers, 1913.

--------. "The Ethnological Analysis of Culture (Presidential Address to Section H of the BAAS)". *Nature*, 87: 356-360, 1911.

--------. "A Genealogical Method of Collecting Social and Vital Statistics". *Journal of the Anthropological Institute of Great Britain and Ireland*, 30: 74-82, 1900.

--------. "The Genealogical Method of Anthropological Inquiry". *Sociological Review*, 3: 1-12, 1910.

--------. "Survival in Sociology". *Sociological Review*, 6: 293-305, 1913.

--------. "The Unity of Anthropology." *Journal of the Royal Anthropological Institute*, 52: 12-25, 1922.

Semple, Ellen Churchill. *Influences of Geographic Environment: On the Basis of Ratzel's System of Anthropo-geography*. New York: H. Holt and Co., 1911.

Schmidt, Wilhelm. *The Culture Historical Method of Ethnology: The Scientific Approach to the Racial Question*. Translated by S. A. Sieber. New York: Fortuny's Publishers, 1939.

--------. *On the Origin of the Idea of God*. New York: Cooper Square Publishers, 1972.

--------. *The Origin and Growth of Religion: Facts and Theories*. Translated by H. J. Rose. London: Methuen, 1931.

Slobodin, Richard. *W.H.R. Rivers*. New York: Columbia University Press, 1978.

Smith, Grafton Elliot. *The Ancient Egyptians and Their Influence upon the Civilisation of Europe*. London: Harper and Brothers, 1923.

--------. *The Ancient Egyptians and the Origin of Civilization.* Freeport, New York: Books for Libraries Press, 1970.

--------. *Conversion in Science.* Great Britain: Richard Clay and Sons, Limited, Bungay, Suffolk, 1929.

--------. *Culture: The Diffusion Controversy.* New York: Norton, 1928.

--------. *The Diffusion of Culture.* London: Watts and Co., 1933.

--------. *Elephants and Ethnologists.* London: Kegan Paul, 1924.

--------. *The Evolution of the Dragon.* Manchester: University of Manchester Press, 1919.

--------. *The Evolution of Man.* Oxford: Oxford University Press, 1927.

--------. *Human History.* London: Cape, 1934.

--------. *In the Beginning: The Origin of Civilisation.* London: Howe, 1932.

--------. *The Influence of Ancient Egyptian Civilization in the East and in America.* Manchester: The University Press, 1916.

--------. *The Migrations of Early Culture.* Manchester: University of Manchester Press, 1929.

--------. *The Place of Thomas Henry Huxley in Anthropology—The Huxley Memorial Lecture for 1935.* London: Royal

Anthropological Institute of Great Britain and Ireland, 1935.

---. *Primitive Men*. London: Oxford University Press, 1916-1917.

---. *The Royal Mummies*. New York: Gerald Duckworth and Co. Ltd., 1912.

---. *Ships as Evidence of the Migrations of Early Culture*. Manchester: Manchester University Press, 1917.

---. *The Significance of the Peking Man*. Edinburgh: The Henderson Trust, 1931.

---. *Tutankhamen and the Discovery of his Tomb by the late Earl of Carnarvon and Mr. Howard Carter*. London: Routledge, 1923.

---. "Anthropological work in Egypt," *Report of the British Association for the Advancement of Science*, 9: 849-850, 1908.

---. "Archaeological Survey of Nubia, Anatomical Report (A)., October 1—December 31, 1908, *Bulletin of the Archaeological Survey of Nubia*, 3: 21-27, 1909.

---. "Archaeological Survey of Nubia, Anatomical Report, January 1—March 31, 1909, *Bulletin of the Archaeological Survey of Nubia*, 4: 19-21, 1909.

---. "The People of Egypt," The Presidential Address of the Cairo Scientific Society, *Cairo Scientific Journal*, v. 3, no. 30: 1-15, 1909.

--------. "Presidential Address to the Anthropological Section, British Association," 11: 575-598, 1912.

--------. "Anthropology," *Encyclopedia Britannica*, 12th edition, new vols. 1, pp. 143-154, London, 1921.

--------. "Edward Burnett Tylor," in Ed. H. J. Massingham. *The Great Victorians*. London: Nicholson and Watson, 1932.

--------. "Foreword," in J. L. Mitchell. *The Conquest of the Maya*. London: Jarrold, 1934.

--------. "Introduction," in H. J. Massingham. *Downland Man*. London: Cape, 1926.

--------. "Preface and Introduction," in John Wilfred Jackson. *Shells as Evidence of the Migrations of Early Culture*. Manchester: Manchester University Press, 1916.

--------. "Preface," in W. H. R. Rivers. *Medicine, Magic and Religion*. London: Kegan Paul, 1924.

--------. "Preface," in C. E. Fox. *The Threshold of the Pacific*. London: Kegan Paul, 1925.

--------, Sir Arthur Keith, F.G. Parsons, M.C. Burkitt, Harold J.E. Peake, and J.L. Myres. *Early Man: His Origin, Development and Culture*. London: E. Benn Limited, 1931.

--------, and W. R. Dawson. *Egyptian Mummies*. London: George Allen and Unwin, 1924.

Wendt, Herbert. *It Began in Babel: The Story of the Birth and

Development of Races and Peoples. Translated by James Kirkup. Boston: Houghton Mifflin, 1962.

White, Leslie A. *The Evolution of Culture—The Development of Civilization to the Fall of Rome*. New York: McGraw-Hill Book Company, Inc., 1959.

Wormington, Hannah Marie. *Ancient Man in North America*. Denver: The Colorado Museum of Natural History, 1939.

Zuckerman, Lord Solly, ed. *The Concepts of Human Evolution: The Proceedings of a Symposium Organized Jointly By the Anatomical Society of Great Britain and Ireland and the Zoological Society of London on 9 and 10 November, 1972*. London: Academic Press, 1973.

Secondary Sources

Anderson, Patricia J. and Jonathan R. Rose. Eds. *British Literary Publishing Houses, 1820-1880.* Detroit: Gale Research, 1991.

Benedict, Ruth. *Patterns of Culture.* Boston: Houghton Mifflin, 1959.

Bernal, Martin. *Black Athena: The Afroasiatic Roots of Classical Civilization.* Volume I. New Brunswick, New Jersey: Rutgers University Press, 1987, 2003.

--------. *Black Athena: The Afroasiatic Roots of Classical Civilization.* Volume II. New Brunswick, New Jersey: Rutgers University Press, 1991.

Barnard, Alan J. *History and Theory in Anthropology.* New York: Cambridge University Press, 2000.

Bidney, David. *Theoretical Anthropology.* New York: Schocken Books, 1967.

Birket-Smith, Kaj. *The Paths of Culture: A General Ethnology.* Translated by Karin Fennow. Madison, Wisconsin: University of Wisconsin Press, 1965.

Blaas, P. B. M. *Continuity and Anachronism: Parliamentary and Constitutional Development in Whig Historiography and in the Anti-Whig Reaction between 1890 and 1930.* The Hague: Martinus Nijhoff, 1978.

Blaut, James Morris. *The Colonizer's Model of the World: Geographical Diffusionism and Eurocentric History.* New

York: Guilford Press, 1993.

Bolt, Christine. *Victorian Attitudes to Race*. London: Routledge and Kegan Paul, 1971.

Bowler, P. J. *The Invention of Progress: The Victorians and the Past*. Oxford: Blackwell, 1989.

--------. *Theories of Human Evolution: A Century of Debate 1844-1944*. Oxford: Blackwell, 1986.

Brace, C. Loring. *The Stages of Human Evolution: Human and Cultural Origins*. Englewood Cliffs, New Jersey: Prentice-Hall, 1988.

Burrow, J. W. *Evolution and Society: A Study in Victorian Social Theory*. Cambridge: Cambridge University Press, 1966.

Butterfield, Herbert. *The Whig Interpretation of History*. London: G. Bell and Sons, 1931.

Cannadine, David. *Ornamentalism: How the British Saw Their Empire*. London: Allen Lane, 2001.

Cavalli-Sforza, Luigi Luca, and Francesco Cavalli-Sforza. *The Great Human Diasporas: The History of Diversity and Evolution*. Translated by Sarah Thorne. Reading, Mass.: Addison-Wesley, 1995.

Chard, Chester S. *Man in Prehistory*. New York: McGraw Hill, 1975.

Dangerfield, George. *The Strange Death of Liberal England*. New

York: Capricorn Books, 1935.

Daniel, Glyn. *150 Years of Archaeology*. Cambridge, Mass.: Harvard University Press, 1975.

Diamond, Jared M. *Guns, Germs, and Steel: The Fates of Human Societies*. New York: W.W. Norton and Company, 1997.

Diop, Cheikh Anta. *The African Origin of Civilization: Myth or Reality*. Translated by Mercer Cook. New York: L. Hill, 1974.

Dorson, R. H. *The British Folklorists: A History*. London: Routledge and Kegan Paul, 1968.

Durham, DeWitt Clinton. "Leo Frobenius and the Reorientation of German Ethnology, 1890-1930." Ph.D. diss., Stanford University, 1985.

Erickson, Paul A. and Liam Donat Murphy. Eds. *A History of Anthropological Theory*. Orchard Park, New York: Broadview Press, 1998.

Evans-Pritchard, Edward. *A History of Anthropological Thought*. New York: Basic Books, 1981.

Gillin, John Phillip. *The Ways of Men: An Introduction to Anthropology*. New York: D. Appleton-Century Co., 1948.

Goodenough, Ward Hunt, Ed. *Explorations in Cultural Anthropology: Essays in Honor of George Peter Murdock*. New York: McGraw-Hill Book Co., 1964.

Goody, Jack. *The Expansive Moment: Anthropology in Britain and Africa, 1917-1970*. New York: Cambridge University Press, 1995.

Harris, Marvin. *The Rise of Anthropological Theory: A History of Theories of Culture*. New York: Crowell, 1968.

--------. *Theories of Culture in Postmodern Times*. Walnut Creek, California: Alta Mira Press, 1999.

Hatch, Elvin. *Theories of Man and Culture*. New York: Columbia University of Press, 1973.

Hearnshaw, L. S. *A Short History of British Psychology, 1840-1940*. London: Methuen Press, 1964.

Hodgen, Margaret T. *Anthropology, History, and Cultural Change*. Tucson: University of Arizona Press, 1974.

Howsam, Leslie. *Kegan Paul—A Victorian Imprint: Publishers, Books and Cultural History*. Toronto: University of Toronto Press, 1998.

Hudson, John C. *Geographical Diffusion Theory: Studies in Geography, No. 19*. Evanston, Ill: Dept. of Geography, 1972.

James, Peter. *Centuries of Darkness: A Challenge to the Conventional Chronology of Old World Archaeology*. New Brunswick, New Jersey: Rutgers University Press, 1993.

Keesing, Roger M. *New Perspectives in Cultural Anthropology*. New York: Holt, Rinehart and Winston, 1971.

King, James C. *The Biology of Race*. New York: Harcourt Brace Jovanovich, 1971.

Koepping, Klaus-Peter. *Adolph Bastian and the Psychic Unity of Mankind: The Foundations of Anthropology in Nineteenth-Century Germany*. New York: The University of Queensland Press, 1985.

Kuklick, Henrika. *The Savage Within: The Social History of British Anthropology, 1885-1945*. New York: Cambridge University Press, 1992.

Kuper, Adam. *Anthropology and Anthropologists: The Modern British School, 1922-1972*. New York: Routledge, 1996.

Lamberg—Karlovsky, C.C., and Jeremy A. Sabloff. *Ancient Civilizations—The Near East and MesoAmerica*. Prospect Heights, Illinois: Waveland Press, Inc., 1987.

Langham, Ian. *The Building of British Social Anthropology: W. H. R. Rivers and His Cambridge Disciples in the Development of Kinship Studies, 1898-1931*. Boston, Mass.: D. Reidel, 1981.

Levine, Philippa. *The Amateur and the Professional: Antiquarians, Historians and Archaeologists in Victorian England 1838-1866*. Cambridge: Cambridge University Press, 1986.

Malchow, Howard L. *Gothic Images of Race in 19th Century Britain*. Stanford, California: Stanford University Press, 1996.

Malefijt, Anne-Marie de Waal. *The Images of Man*. New York: Alfred A. Knopf, 1974.

Mundkur, Balaji. *The Cult of the Serpent—An Interdisciplinary Survey of Its Manifestations and Origins.* Albany: State University of New York Press, 1983.

Naroll, Raoul, and Frada Naroll. *Main Currents in Cultural Anthropology.* Englewood Cliffs, New Jersey: N.J. Prentice-Hall, 1973.

Poe, Richard. *Black Spark, White Fire: Did African Explorers Civilize Ancient Europe?.* Rocklin, California: Prima Publishing, 1997.

Quigley, Carroll. *The Evolution of Civilizations: An Introduction to Historical Analysis.* New York: MacMillan, 1961.

Renfrew, Colin. *Approaches to Social Archaeology.* Cambridge, Mass.: Harvard University Press, 1984.

--------. *British Prehistory: A New Outline.* Park Ridge, New Jersey: Noyes Press, 1975.

--------. *The Emergence of Civilisation: The Cyclades and the Aegean in the 3rd Millennium B.C.* London: Methuen, 1972.

Richards, Graham D. "William Halse Rivers (1864-1922)." *The Psychologist* 14, no. 9 (September 2001): 464.

Riley, Carroll L., Ed. *Man Across the Sea—The Problems of Pre-Columbian Contacts.* Austin: University of Texas Press, 1971.

Rogers, Everett M. *Communication of Innovations: A Cross Cultural Approach.* New York: Free Press, 1971.

--------. *Diffusion of Innovations.* New York: Free Press, 1983.

Rothblatt, Sheldon. *The Revolution of the Dons: Cambridge Society in Victorian England.* London: Faber, 1968.

Rouse, Irving. *Introduction to Prehistory: A Systematic Approach.* New York: McGraw-Hill, 1972.

Said, Edward. *Orientalism.* New York: Vintage Books, 1979.

Schorske, Carl. *Thinking with History: Explorations in the Passage to Modernism.* Princeton, New Jersey: Princeton University Press, 1998.

Sowell, Thomas. *Conquests and Cultures: An International History.* New York: Basic Books, 1998.

--------. *Migrations and Cultures: A World View.* New York: Basic Books, 1996.

Stringer, Chris, and Robin McKie. *African Exodus.* New York: Henry Holt, 1997.

Stocking, Jr., George W. Ed. *After Tylor: British Social Anthropology, 1888-1951.* Madison, Wisconsin: University of Wisconsin Press, 1995.

--------. *Functionalism Historicized: Essays on British Social Anthropology.* v. II. Madison, Wisconsin: University of Wisconsin Press, 1984.

--------. *Objects and Others: Essays on Museums and Material*

Culture. Madison, Wisconsin: University of Wisconsin Press, 1985.

--------. *Victorian Anthropology*. New York: The Free Press, 1991.

Thompson, Richard L., and Michael A. Cremo. *Forbidden Archeology: The Hidden History of the Human Race*. Los Angeles: Bhaktivedanta Book Publishing, 1998.

Titiev, Mischa. *The Science of Man*. New York: Holt, Rinehart and Winston, 1963.

Trigger, Bruce G. *A History of Archaeological Thought*. New York: Cambridge University Press, 1989.

Urry, James. *Before Social Anthropology: Essays on the History of British Anthropology*. Reading: Harwood Academic Publishers, 1993.

Vermeulen, Hans F. and Arturo Alvarez Roldan. *Fieldwork and Footnotes: Studies in the History of European Anthropology*. New York: Routledge, 1995.

Voget, Fred. *A History of Ethnology*. New York: Holt, Rinehart and Winston, 1975.

Whittle, Paul. "W. H. R. Rivers: A Founding Father Worth Remembering," *Science as Culture*, Department of Experimental Psychology, University of Cambridge, http://human-nature.com/science-as-culture/whittle.html.

Index

A
Africa
    39, 72, 75, 77, 80, 109-110, 114, 118
Agriculture
    43, 59, 61, 63, 93, 105
America(-as)
    44, 51, 58, 62, 71-72, 78-79, 96, 116
Anatomy
    12, 19-22, 65, 69, 108, 110
Anthropology(-ists, -ical)
    7-17, 19, 22-29, 31-34, 39-44, 47-48, 50-51, 55, 57-58, 60-61, 65-68, 71-73, 77-92, 95, 100, 108-114, 116-120
Arabia
    80
Arch(a)eology
    8, 34, 39, 42, 50, 54, 98, 112, 118
Aristotle
    29, 76, 103, 106
Asia (Asiatic)
    29, 31, 72, 78-79, 93, 97

B
Babylonian
    31, 59, 78, 80, 91
Bacon, Francis
    106
Barbarian(-ism)
    26, 28, 75, 103
Bastian, Adolph
    33-36, 45-53, 55, 73

Biology
> 19, 52

Boas, Franz
> 33, 44

British
> 7-9, 11-13, 15, 18, 20-21, 23, 25, 30, 32-33, 35, 38, 43, 46, 50, 52, 59-60, 65, 72-73, 80, 82-83, 87-89, 91-95, 97, 101, 109-110, 116-119

C

Cartesianism
> 49, 75-76, 106

Catastrophism
> 100

Civilization (Civilisation)
> 7-10, 12, 19, 23, 26-27, 29-31, 36, 39, 41-43, 46, 52-53, 55, 60-63, 65-66, 69-71, 75-76, 79, 83, 88-95, 98, 102, 104-106

Classicism (Classicists)
> 58-59

Comte, Auguste
> 47-49, 76, 84

Crete
> 78-79

Cultural anthropology
> 22-23, 25, 65

Cultural evolution
> 16, 50, 76

Culture(-s)
> 7-9, 16, 19, 23, 27, 33-37, 40-41, 44, 49-53, 56-57, 60-66, 69-71, 73, 75-80, 83, 89, 91-92, 94, 96, 98, 102, 104, 112-113, 118-119

D

Descartes
> 76, 106

Determinist
> 75-77, 98, 118

Development
    10-11, 15-16, 24, 26-27, 40, 42, 44, 48, 61-62, 67, 75, 94, 97, 101, 118
Diffusionism
    7, 9, 11, 13, 15, 23, 25, 29, 32-35, 37, 39-41, 43-44, 55, 57-58, 61, 64, 68, 74, 77, 81, 86, 88-89, 93, 97-98, 112, 118-120
Diffusionists
    9, 11-14, 16-17, 23, 25-36, 39, 41-46, 50-53, 55, 57-61, 65, 70, 72-75, 80, 83, 85-86, 88-102, 105, 107-108, 110-113, 116, 118-119
Durkheim, Emile
    49, 85-87
Dynamic
    84, 118

E

Egyptocentric
    12, 25, 72
Egyptology
    8, 38, 114
Enlightenment
    48-49
Essentialist
    70
Ethnicity
    77-78, 98
Ethnography
    8, 46
Ethnology
    7-8, 12, 14-15, 23, 30, 33-35, 46-48, 54-55, 89, 91, 98
Eugenics
    27-28
Evolution(-ism, -ary)
    7, 15-20, 24, 26-29, 33, 35-36, 40, 43-44, 46, 48-55, 58, 60, 66-67, 72-74, 76, 80-84, 86-87, 89, 94, 102, 117
Ex Oriente Lux
    41-42

F
Frazerian
  86
Funding
  7, 25, 106-111, 115-116, 118
G
Galen
  76, 106
Galileo
  74, 76, 106
Genealogical (-ies)
  14-15, 24, 85, 96
H
Heliocentric
  7
Heliolithic
  7-9, 13, 25, 28-29, 35, 37, 40, 42-44, 56, 58, 60, 65, 70, 79, 88, 92-95, 97-99, 102-103, 105, 107, 112-113, 119
Herodotus
  29
History
  7, 13, 18-19, 22-23, 25, 27, 29, 34, 38, 51-52, 54, 57, 63, 69, 71, 74-76, 80, 82-83, 86, 89-91, 93, 96, 102, 105, 108, 112
Historicist
  89, 111, 113, 117-118
Humanism(-ists)
  50, 75-76
Huxley, T.H.
  20, 66-70
I
Independent invention (development)
  34, 45, 50, 52, 55, 117
India
  14, 31, 57, 62, 65, 78-80, 95, 98, 100-101

Indonesia
	23, 56-57, 60, 91, 97
Isolationism
	11, 75, 89
Isolationists
	68, 119

J

Jackson, John W.
	57

K

Kuklick, Henrika
	83, 109, 116
Kulturkreis
	34, 44, 73
Kuper, Adam
	16, 39, 83, 86, 88

L

Le Mirage Oriental
	41
Linguistics
	8, 29-30, 32-33, 57
Locke, John
	103-104
London School of Economics (LSE)
	86, 109-111, 115-116

M

Malinowski, Bronislaw
	16, 55, 84-87, 92, 109-111, 114-118
Materialist
	12
Megalithic
	7, 23, 56-57, 60, 88-89
Melanesia
	17-18, 23, 40, 57, 90
Middle East
	9, 59

Migration
    29, 35, 41, 57, 88, 91, 96-97, 114
Monogenist
    46
Multilinear (multilineal)
    46, 89

N
Natural Man
    102
Neurology
    12, 14, 66, 69
Nilotic
    64, 70
Nubia
    21

O
Oceania
    62, 78-79

P
Paleoanthropology
    12
Paleontology
    19-20, 98, 100
Paradigm
    15, 26, 109, 112, 117-118
Peking
    98
Petrie, W. M. F.
    38, 41, 43
Phoenicia(-ns)
    79, 95
Physical anthropology
    8, 32, 85
Plato (Neo-Platonism)
    29, 51

Polygenism(-ist)
 30, 46
Positivism
 48-50, 75, 110
Post-processualism
 12
Pre-Columbian
 10, 78
Prehistory
 8, 19, 47, 80, 101
Presentist
 12, 44, 112, 116-118
Processualism
 12
Professionalization
 7-8, 15, 118
Progress(-ivism, -ivists)
 19, 24, 26-29, 44, 75-76, 94, 106
Psychiatry(-ist)
 12, 16, 52
Psychic unity
 34-35, 46-47, 50-52, 75-76
Psychology(-ist, -ical)
 12, 14-15, 18, 24, 39, 47, 52, 55, 63, 73, 81-82, 84, 102, 105
Ptolemy
 76, 106

R

Radcliffe-Brown, A.R.
 15, 84-87, 111, 115-117
Radiocarbon (Carbon-14 or C-14)
 8, 13, 25, 113-114
Ratzel, Friedrich
 34-35, 44, 97
Reductionist
 119

Romanticism
    48-49
Rosetta stone
    38

S

Savage(-ry)
    26, 48, 103
Scientism
    12, 50
Serpent cult(s)
    57, 80, 95
Shell shock syndrome (Post-traumatic stress disorder, PTSD)
    17
Social anthropology
    8, 12, 15, 25, 27, 109, 112
Social Darwinism
    26-27, 53, 77
Sociology of Scientific Knowledge
    10
Specialization
    8, 118
Static
    32, 84, 87, 118
Sumer
    31, 62, 71, 79
Sun
    7, 57, 59, 60-62, 69, 80, 88

T

Transoceanic
    10-11, 78
Trigger, Bruce
    34, 42, 112, 114-115
Tylor, E.B.
    34, 44, 86
Typology(-ical)
    70, 94, 119

U
Unilinear (unilineal)
　　15-16, 24, 44, 54, 83, 89, 94, 117
University College, London (UCL)
　　12, 21-24, 55, 65, 103, 107-111
V
Victorian
　　26-27, 107
Voltaire
　　50, 106
W
World War I
　　16, 26, 27, 63
World War II (Second World War)
　　42, 110, 112
Wittgenstein, Ludwig
　　55

Dedicated to my mother who has touched so many lives and has made this series possible due to unwavering encouragement.

I also wish to offer special appreciation to my family and friends.

www.ingramcontent.com/pod-product-compliance
Lightning Source LLC
Chambersburg PA
CBHW031358040426
42444CB00005B/334